REDEMPTION AND RESPONSIBILITY:

A FEW HOURS WITH GEORGE ALDER

Edited by
Mick Bollenbaugh
and Gary Tiffin

RESOURCE *Publications* • Eugene, Oregon

Permission to reprint these articles which first appeared in The Lookout magazine, has been kindly granted by The Lookout magazine and its publisher, Standard Publishing of Cincinnati, Ohio.

Copyright©2000 by the Alder Family.

ISBN: 1-57910-323-5

Printed by *Wipf & Stock Publishers*, 2000.

Contents

CHAPTER ONE: THE BIBLE 7

CHAPTER TWO: DAILY LIFE 25

CHAPTER THREE: THE CHURCH 47

CHAPTER FOUR: DOCTRINE 63

CHAPTER FIVE: PRACTICAL LIVING 81

CHAPTER SIX: SOCIAL ISSUES 103

CHAPTER SEVEN: GOVERNMENT-THE NATION 127

CHAPTER EIGHT: GOD'S WORLD 147

CHAPTER NINE: THE SEASONS 161

CHAPTER TEN: MORTALITY AND HOPE 175

PREFACE

This book is late. Even before George died in 1986, he and Eileen had made inquiries about the possibility of publishing an edited version of his more than fifteen years of weekly columns titled "A Minute With George Alder"—which appeared in The Lookout between 1968 and 1985.

We were both George's students, deeply and indelibly influenced by his teaching, presence, balance, precise logic, and unfaltering commitment to Scripture and its sane application to our world today. Mick was a student from 1971-75. Gary was a student from 1958-62, and then a faculty colleague from 1965-72. As we reread all 750 columns, struggling to decide which to include and how to organize them, we were reminded of the breadth of George's wisdom, learning, and common sense. He was ahead of his time in so many ways: He called for a responsible use of the environment long before it became politically correct among mainstream evangelical Christians; he rejoiced in the growing role women were playing in the life of the church, even as many resisted; he early discerned the danger of automatically linking conservative politics to Christianity, even though his articles attest to a fundamental conservatism, e.g. abortion, law and order, and government. A patriot at heart, George nevertheless echoes the prophets in his call for a passionate justice and ethic in the land.

Every president under whom he served at San Jose Christian College recognized that George was the de facto leader of the faculty, and leaned heavily upon his counsel and wisdom. His interest in the affairs of this world was surpassed by his dogged commitment to his Lord, Church, and family. He encouraged and challenged. He provoked and cared. He discovered and helped others do the same. His love for the outdoors and the High Sierras was close to his love for the integrity of the Christian life to which he aspired—and which he exemplified so well.

In 1964, George considered pursuing a Stanford Ph.D. degree, but decided that family and career commitments made such a decision untenable. As two of his students who did take that pathway, we witness to the fact that there is a wisdom not attainable through doctoral programs; there is a learning beyond the classroom; and there are a few like George for whom doctoral study would not have advanced stature much.

Born August 20, 1920, in Thorp, Washington, George was the middle child of a tenant farming family in the Ellensburg, Washington, area. In 1944, after one year at Central Washington College of Education, George transferred to Northwest Christian College to study for ministry. He graduated from both NCC and the University of Oregon (majoring in Greek). He later completed an M.A. in Speech and Drama at San Jose State University, where he served as an adjunct professor of speech for many years, in addition to his long-time teaching career at San Jose Christian College.

From an early preaching ministry, George, Eileen and their five children moved to San Jose, California, in 1954 to begin a 28 year teaching ministry at San Jose Christian College, serving under Presidents Bill Jessup, Al Tiffin, Woody Phillips, and Charles Boatman. He taught a wide range of courses including Greek, Logic, Literature, New Testament, Speech, and Basic Christian Faith. His impressive personal library always inspired us to read more. George and Eileen returned to Oregon in 1981 to live near Mollala where he spent significant time writing and conducting seminars on ecology for the Institute for Christian Resources. When George became aware of his inoperable cancer in 1984, he and Eileen moved to Turner, Oregon, where Eileen still resides, surrounded by the love of longtime colleagues and friends.

This volume is dedicated to Eileen, whose contributions to student lives were usually unseen, but always obvious to those who knew her well.

We present this compilation of George's thinking as representatives of the hundreds of students who love him and honor his memory today by continuing service for Christ all over the United States and around the world. We believe you will be pleased to spend "many minutes" with George in this volume.

Mick Bollenbaugh & Gary Tiffin
December 1999
Northwest Christian College - Eugene, Oregon

CHAPTER ONE

THE BIBLE

George Alder was speaking at a Crossbearer's Crusade at San Jose Bible College in 1971. At the outdoor worship service he preached entirely without notes, employing only his own Greek New Testament. Such deep familiarity with the Bible, especially in one of its original languages, was not lost even on an eighteen-year-old.

George's ability with the Koine Greek of the New Testament was a means to a greater end, namely to understand and put into practice the message of the Bible. In other words, George was aware of the potential for pride because one could say he or she "knows" Greek. On more than one occasion Professor Alder had to clip the wings of those whose immaturity was getting the best of them by their thinking some distinct advantage had been gained by "learning" Greek. He was quick to remind us that humility, not pride, was a central message in the Bible. If we did not learn this lesson, all the Greek in the world would do us no good. He was cognizant of the fact that an ability in a Biblical language might cause us to attempt to dazzle or intimidate those uninitiated in Greek or Hebrew. Hence, as George says in one of the articles in this section, we must "demythologize Greek." An uncritical adoption of such phrases as "the Greek says" could tempt us to become Biblical elitists who might dishonestly advance our pet theological causes. George refused to yield to these temptations. For him Greek was useful only to the extent that it motivates a deeper study of the Bible.

The truth is that George forgot more Greek than most of us will ever know. Yet after more than four decades of teaching Greek, George thought of himself as still learning the language. He was the rare combination of a person who approached Scripture with academic integrity and in an attitude of reverence.

What's It Worth?

August 6, 1972

Several years ago Christies, the great London art auction house, received a painting from the eighty-two-year-old widow of a picture framer. It was a painting of the classic myth, The Judgment of Paris. The picture framer had paid $2 for it. Christies attributed it to a seventeenth-century copyist, appraised it at $280, and put it on sale. Oliver Miller, deputy surveyor of the Queen's paintings, recognized it as an original Rubens and the price went up to $280,000.

How swiftly the value changed once the expert had properly identified it! The value was always there. Man's ignorance did not change the picture into anything but a Rubens.

How often the values of the Bible are missed because the judge is incompetent to assess the value. When Robert Owen, nineteenth-century industrialist, social planner, and skeptic was twelve years old he read the Bible and decided that it wasn't worth anything. He lived and died accepting the immature judgment of a twelve-year-old boy about the Bible.

An American having stormed through a great European art gallery passed judgment at the door, "There isn't a thing worth seeing in here!" The doorman put him down, "Sir, these paintings are not on trial, the spectators are!"

The Bible is not really on trial before its human critics. The present rediscovery of its great message among many people is testimony, not to any change in the message, but to a change in people. A painting worth $280,000 can be sold for $2 only because of the abysmal ignorance of those who look upon it. Have you consigned the Bible to a place upon a shelf while searching madly for life's answers elsewhere?

A Bible in the Mind?

June 17, 1973

One of the really thrilling stories coming back with our POW's from Vietnam was reported in the March 12 issue of *Time*. In one of the prison camps the men attempted to put a Bible together from memory. Everyone contributed the verses he could recall from the Word so that they would have a Bible for study and worship services.

Personal religious faith expressed in this collective way helped to sustain these men through some of the bitterest trials known to human beings. Air Force Major Norman McDaniel said, "Most of my fellow-prisoners had faith in God. When the going got tough, then came the test to see if we were worthy."

The psalmist said, "Thy word have I treasured in my heart, that I might not sin against thee . . . I shall delight in thy statutes; I shall not forget thy word" (Psalm 119:11, 16). Perhaps the testimony of the POW's will prove a stimulus to Christians to study God's Word more and to memorize more of it. What if your congregation had to produce a Bible from memory? How complete would it be? Would the treasure house of the collective memory be filled with verses, paragraphs, chapters, and even books?

Obviously, this is not some kind of ultimate measurement of spiritual virtue or maturity. We do know, however, that whatever really interests us we will fix in memory. The man who loves baseball will give you scores, names, batting averages, and the outcome of World Series contests for years past. The photography hobbyist can recite all kinds of technical data about his hobby. The automobile enthusiast knows displacements, suspensions, gear ratios, and a ton of other factual things about cars.

Isn't it reasonable then to expect that if a Christian puts the Bible at the very center of his reading and study he will just naturally come to know many verses, paragraphs, chapters, and books almost by heart?

Jesus quoted Scripture in the wilderness of temptation, in His discussions with the Pharisees and scribes, in teaching His disciples, and in His agony on the cross. He is our example, and He memorized Scripture. Shouldn't we?

"It's All in the Bible." Is It?

March 24, 1974

We used to have a challenging slogan board in the foyer of the administration building of our college. A new quote or slogan would appear there each week. I was surprised one day to see: "A house divided against itself cannot stand."—A. Lincoln. I thought that just everybody knew that Jesus said that and that Lincoln was borrowing. Reflecting further I remembered a dear lady in a country church who thought that "Now I lay me down to sleep . . ." was the Lord's Prayer. That was an error on the other side. And I guess you could fool a lot of people with "Cleanliness is next to godliness."

Well, what really concerns me about this kind of thing is that many people assume things about the Bible that just aren't so. Biblical support for interpretations of various events is labeled, "It's all in the Bible," or "The Bible is being fulfilled," or "Undoubtedly this fulfills Scripture." Time and time again I've heard "There shall be wars and rumors of wars" quoted as if this meant that modern strife fulfills Jesus' words and therefore He is about to come! Actually, He had just warned His disciples against being misled this way. "The end is not yet," He said (Matthew 24:6). If you look at the whole passage you'll see that He was talking about the destruction of Jerusalem.

Simply to quote or refer to the Bible in connection with modern events, or past or future events for that matter, does not necessarily mean that this is what the Bible is talking about.

The David Wilkerson film "The Road to Armageddon" is an example of this. The implication in the title is that we are on the road to a great war called Armageddon. Over and over Wilkerson states this and claims that the Bible supports his view, although he scarcely quotes the Bible. At the end of the film he says that these conclusions were revealed to him in a dream.

When someone claims "It's in the Bible," let's require that he show us; otherwise, we may subscribe to a lot of nonsense that isn't in the Bible at all.

Where's the Edge?

April 4, 1976

"It's too bad, isn't it," she said, "that we make so much fuss over little minor differences in how we understand the Bible?" Now what's the answer? Am I to say, "Sure, we shouldn't worry about little things"? Or do I point out that many times what people call "minor differences" may in fact be quite important from a Biblical point of view?

The case in point was whether sprinkling, pouring, or immersion was Bible baptism. So I had to discuss the difference between petty human differences and clear Bible teachings. The teachings of the Bible could all be set aside if we would simply consider that matters people differ about are matters of little consequence.

Maybe we can better understand this problem by thinking of ourselves on the top of a mountain with cliffs breaking off all around. This is the mountaintop of Bible doctrine. It is quite large. There is a lot of room to roam and investigate. There is considerable room to differ with others on many things. But the mountain is surrounded by those dangerous cliffs. These are the edges where we drop off. Knowing the fundamental Bible teachings provides warning about the edges. For example, we may vary in our thinking about the relationship of the divine and the human in Jesus, but we fall over the cliff when we say, "He's all divine" or, "He's only human."

Careful study of the Bible provides the safety fences at the cliff's edge. Appreciation of the Word gives us the whole mountain to roam. But we'd better be careful that we don't look at the safety fences and say, "The cliffs really aren't there, are they? It's silly to worry about them."

Two Million Dollars for a Book!

June 4, 1978

In early April, a Gutenberg Bible was auctioned for two million dollars. The book dealer who bought it hopes to sell it again at a profit, and he probably will. He didn't buy it for the content, but for the fact that it is one of only twenty-six such Bibles in the world. It is a rare edition of the first book printed in moveable type.

It is significant that Gutenberg's project was a Bible, not a copy of Plato's dialogues, Homer's epic poems, or Cicero's orations. The Bible was considered to be the most valuable book and the most desired one when that first venture in printing took place.

Now for very little money one can buy a simple paperbound Bible in any of hundreds of different languages. More dedicated human effort continues to be given to the reproduction of this Book than to any other.

It really isn't the two million dollars spent for one, or a dollar spent for another that adequately measures the value of this Book. Its content opens to man a treasure beyond all earth's wealth. There are no scales to weigh the worth of the revelation that God is love, that He is the Creator, that Jesus, His Son, is our Savior, and that in Him we have eternal life.

We needn't spend a lot of money to possess this Book that holds the key to coffers holding treasures beyond human imagination. But to enjoy the riches, we must use the Book, read it, study it, act upon its instructions, and live in obedience to its guidance and laws.

If you could get a Bible only by selling all you have, would you make that sale and buy the treasured Book?

Mushrooms and Verses

July 23, 1978

I've liked mushrooms for a long time but I've not studied mushrooms enough to know which are poisonous and which aren't. I would never go into the woods and fields with confidence to gather them. After all, the threat of getting poisoned for one's ignorance is a strong deterrent to hunting mushrooms. Of course, I know that there are people who know all about mushrooms, and they'll say that it really isn't so hard to learn how to tell them apart. Still I haven't ventured to become a gatherer, just because I like to eat them. That desire could get me killed.

Repayment for error is not swift nor immediately fatal (usually) for those who gather Bible verses for guidance without careful study. Therefore many people use the Bible like a blind man hungry for mushrooms, gathering them by touch alone. Without any knowledge of a verse's context, culture, or original language, they walk in blindness. They pick Bible verses for their pleasant-sounding words or because they seem to fit the situation. It's easy for them to see, for example, that Jesus healed people. Since they would like to be well, they might easily reach the unwarranted conclusion that any sick person can be cured if only he'll be a true Christian.

A person who walks through the fields and forest glades of Scripture, gathering proof texts as he goes, may endanger his soul's health as surely as an unwary, untrained mushroom gatherer endangers his life, and maybe the lives of others.

No Bible verse in itself will poison a soul, but misused texts can so misguide that soon the whole Bible becomes a confusion. Instead of guidance for the soul, it becomes support for misdirection. We ought to apply at least as much diligence to gathering Bible verses as we do to mushrooms.

Eros or Agape?

September 3, 1978

When we talk of love, we commonly think of it in the Bible sense. We know that the Bible's love is *agape*, a higher form of love than was generally known in the ancient world. It is instructive to realize that the word most often used among the Greeks for love, *eros*, is not used at all in the New Testament. The basic distinction between the two words explains why this is so.

The Greeks believed that reflection, the ability of the mind to evaluate, was the highest mental gift. But passion, or *eros*, put an end to reflection and lifted man upward in a passionate hunger for God. Religion and ecstasy were joined together as a transport to take man beyond his rationality. Therefore, the Greeks and others in the ancient world developed all kinds of licentious worship practices.

Eros is a love that seeks its own gratification. It is drawn toward its object seeking to find in others its own life fulfillment. But *agape* is just the opposite of this. This is a giving love that operates not from impulse, but from a sense of responsibility. It is love that seeks to bring its gifts to others rather than draw its satisfaction from others.

John says that "God is love" and tells us that "we love, because He first loved us." It is because of His giving to us that we learn to respond in giving to Him and to others. Any attempt to use others or God for our own purpose is a violation of *agape* and a return to *eros*.

We are always being tested in the tension between the poles of *eros* and *agape*. In childhood we seek in others the fulfillment of our own needs. In maturity we become givers. So Paul says that beyond all demonstrations of personal gifts, the most important and more excellent way is love.

Why Study the Old Testament?

January 22, 1984

Pick up your Bible and open it at the division between the Old and the New Testaments, at the end of Malachi and the beginning of Matthew.

In the Bible I'm holding, that puts 907 pages in the Old Testament and 270 pages in the New Testament. So that's 77 percent Old Testament and 23 percent New Testament.

We know that we are now under the teachings of the New Testament, so why do we need to study that other 77 percent of the Bible?

In the first place, it is in the Old Testament that we learn about God's plan for our salvation in Jesus. We can trace His family line through the Old Testament. It is this bloodline of the Messiah that gives unity to the message of the Old Testament.

Second, a lot of Old Testament passages are either quoted or alluded to in the New Testament. To discover the contexts for these verses, we need to understand the surrounding passages in the Old Testament. We can't, for example, understand how Jesus is our high priest unless we know something of this office as it is described in Leviticus.

Third, many, many errors in Biblical understanding come about because people mix up the Old and New Covenants. We are a New-Covenant people. The Old Covenant has been abrogated by the New. The implications of this are lost to those who do not understand the Old Testament.

Fourth, we are told by Paul that incidents in the Old Testament are "examples" for us. We learn about life by observing how God dealt with His people under the Old Covenant. Think of the encouragement we derive from the heroes of the faith as they are described briefly in the eleventh chapter of Hebrews. David going out to meet Goliath is an example of what it means to trust God regardless of the nature of the opposition.

Fifth, books like the Psalms, Proverbs, and Ecclesiastes allow us to participate in the religious experience of others. From these books we learn that life is tough and that God is good. We are comforted and strengthened by the expressions of praise, love, and faith toward God given in this section of the Bible, and we are instructed as well in the practical things of everyday living. Amos and other prophets teach us that religion must be vital and not simply a routine fulfillment of rituals.

Sixth, the great prophetic passages that predict the coming of Jesus serve to establish our faith in Him as God's Son. Matthew quotes many of these prophecies to prove to the Jews that the Messiah had come.

Many other reasons can be cited for studying the Old Testament. These six should encourage us not to rely upon a lightweight Bible, leaving out those first 907 pages. They are the foundation and the prelude to the other 270 pages that we know as the New Testament. We need the whole Bible.

The Bible or Experience?

March 4, 1984

It was hard to believe I had heard what I'd heard: "I know that's what the Bible teaches," the woman said, "but that's not the way I was saved." This completely assured theological statement followed two hours of studying together what the Bible teaches about how to be saved. The woman had affirmed Scripture after Scripture. She never questioned Jesus' authority or the authority of His apostles. She didn't question the command to be baptized. But she was confident that the Lord had saved her in a manner different from that given in the Bible.

If one follows experience as the ultimate guide in theology, then of course one becomes the law to himself. A very dominant or charismatic person may impose his views on others who will follow him and affirm that his experience is the norm for the group. All in the group must affirm this experience and testify to their participation in it. Denominations are often formed in just this way.

When I was a little boy, I attended a Sunday school class in an experience-oriented church. Our teacher taught us that we'd know we were saved when we had some kind of experience. We were told to pray for this. I prayed. I was frustrated and disappointed. Nothing happened to assure me of God's favor. I did not have the desired experiential witness of salvation. That was disquieting, even somewhat frightening.

When I learned to depend upon the clear teaching of Scripture and to act upon this teaching, then I received assurance. Then I knew that I was saved because of what Christ had done for me and because of what the Bible told me about the way to be saved.

Such assurance is a good experience. But it is the assurance that provides the experience, not the other way around.

Often it is very difficult to move a person from depending upon personal experience as validation of God's special favor in that person's life. One who persists in the experientially validated assurance of acceptance will often be disappointed when experience is not positive but very negative—illness, defeat, alienation.

When, however, we have learned to trust in Him as He teaches us in His Word, then we have an unchanging basis for assurance. That's a good experience.

Maybe we should not say, then, "The Bible or Experience," but rather "The Bible *and* Experience."

Demythologizing Greek

March 31, 1985

Have you ever been intimidated by a teacher or preacher who confidently affirmed, "The Greek says..."? Most of us have been in this position. If we aren't scholars in the Greek language, how can we know whether what the speaker is saying "the Greek says" is true? Not much of a chance for us to question the authority of the Greek, is there?

Well, I have news for you. You don't need to study Greek to defend yourself, nor do you need to be intimidated by "the Greek says." What you need to know is the mythology around this language.

At one time even many scholars were deluded into thinking that the Greek of the New Testament was a special kind of Holy Spirit language, something designed just for the Word of God. Consequently, knowledge of this language was very special, an almost priestly power held only by the few who were enlightened.

Later on, abundant evidence was found to show that the Greek of the New Testament was primarily just the common language of the people, like everyday English is our common language now.

But what are these myths that have grown up around the Greek and continue to be perpetuated by well-meaning, if mistaken, experts on this language? First, "Greek is the most accurate language." Well, even if that could be proven, it wouldn't mean much. All languages are by nature inaccurate. Greek is no different from other languages in this respect. It's filled with problems for the scholars. Ideas cannot be expounded in Greek with anything approaching 100 percent accuracy.

Second, "Greek always has a special, exact word for everything, whereas English uses the same word for many things." Not true. The whole vocabulary of the New Testament is only about five thousand words. That's about the same size vocabulary as we have in everyday spoken English. Many words in both Greek and English have to serve in a number of different ways. Greek is no more dedicated than English to matching words precisely, without ambiguity, to either things or ideas.

Third, "Greek has very exact grammatical rules; English is sloppy." Mythology again. The rules of grammar are descriptions of the way things generally work; they are not accepted laws handed down to make things work as they do. So we write rules and then we write exceptions to the rules because the rules only describe; they don't control languages or the people who speak them.

Fourth, "Without Greek we cannot really understand the New Testament." False! The translations are very good. All the important information comes through quite easily.

Fifth, "Many important texts are not translated correctly." Often we hear this from someone who is grinding a personal theological axe. He knows he can succeed only by making his own unique translation. Beware!

Mind you, I'd be the last to say that an understanding of Greek is not helpful, even very valuable and rewarding, in Bible study for the earnest student. I've been at this study for forty-two years as a college teacher of Greek. However, much of what I've heard confidently affirmed in public about Greek has been wrong, a part of the mythology that has grown on the language like mistletoe on oak trees.

Don't be intimidated by this mythology. Obviously, it is unfair of those who know little (or much) of the Greek to stifle discussion by pontificating about what the Greek says. It's even more unfair to use such knowledge to advance uniquely private interpretations.

Most of us can recognize credible scholarship. This is marked by humility, recognition that tough problems have more than one side, willingness to listen, caution in making sweeping affirmations, lack of defensiveness when questioned, and an openness to the ideas of others. Above all, credible scholarship is marked by a deep desire to know God's Word and to follow it. Credible scholarship does not manufacture or perpetuate mythology.

More on Demythologizing Greek

April 14, 1985

Several weeks ago (March 31) I discussed the mythology that has grown up around the Greek language, particularly among Bible believers. Now I'd like to share a few examples of arguments based upon the Greek that sound good until the facts are known.

Some years ago I heard a well-educated, conscientious brother (I mean that sincerely) discussing John 3:3-5. He pointed out that being born of water and the Spirit was like a human birth, requiring both male and female elements. The Spirit, he confidently assured us, is the masculine element, and the water is the feminine element. He substantiated this argument by saying that *spirit* in the Greek language is a masculine noun and *water* is a feminine noun. So what's the problem? Both nouns are grammatically neuter nouns! A little research could have saved my friend from this blunder. Unfortunately, many people would just accept this argument as another of those remarkable "the Greek says" illuminations.

Or think about this: In a rather convoluted argument about marriage and divorce, a preacher asserted that his explanation of certain texts took into account some vital information that the translators had missed or suppressed. He explained that the translators had missed the vital truth that *gyne* should be translated *woman* and that *gynekos* should be rendered *wife*, or was it the other way around? That sounds pretty powerful in an argument before an audience that doesn't know Greek. So, again, what's the problem?

Gyne and *gynekos* are the same word. They are declensional forms that show how the word is used. This argument is comparable to claiming that *mice* and *mouse* are different words. *Gyne* means *woman*, but is also used for *wife*.

Problems of this kind develop because sometimes people who know a little about Greek have accepted some mythology about the precision of Greek, and then they become too sure of themselves, drawing conclusions from ideas that are not accurate.

Of course, I can cite many examples of insights gained from an understanding of the Greek. In any language there are nuances that are difficult to translate, so that a thorough knowledge of the language may provide a lot of delightful and rewarding information. But we need to be cautious, even skeptical, about big pronouncements based upon Greek. It is very easy to go astray.

Finally, knowledge of Greek seldom actually solves any tough Scriptural problems. But careful study of the Greek will help us to understand what the problems are. There are, for sure, some obscurities and difficulties in our English translations that become plain right away when we know the Greek.

It seems wise to me for those who study Greek to use whatever expertise they develop as a tool for explaining things in English, not as a club to dominate others or to stifle debate. After all, when I make a piece of furniture in my workshop, it is the piece of furniture that I show to others, not my workshop or my tools. Greek is a marvelous tool when used knowledgeably, just as a table saw is great for furniture construction. Either can be treacherous when used carelessly.

Common (Koine) Greek

April 21, 1985

In 356 B.C., Alexander, later called the Great, was born. His name continues in cities such as Alexandria, Egypt. His father, Philip of Macedon, gave his name to Philippi when he captured the site from the Thaseans. Another famous New Testament city, Thessalonica, is named for Alexander's sister.

Alexander grew up in Macedon, an area looked upon by the southern, sophisticated Athenians as uncultured, almost barbarian. Philip, however, desired a good education for his son, so he ordered Aristotle to come to Macedon to be Alexander's private tutor. This was like bringing a whole university to Macedon, because among the Greeks Aristotle was recognized as the foremost philosopher, educator, scientist, rhetorician, literary critic, and political scientist.

So Alexander received the best education possible. Central to this education was the memorization of the entire *Iliad* and *Odyssey*, the great and lengthy epic poems of Homer. These poems, Aristotle, and some other important Greek thinkers influenced the young Alexander to dream of a world united under the discipline and direction of Greek culture.

When at age twenty Alexander became king, he launched a vigorous, unprecedented expansion program for the next twelve years until his death. In that time he accomplished his dream, lamenting that there were no more worlds to conquer. Perhaps his greatest legacy to us is the language of the New Testament, now called "koine" Greek.

Everywhere Alexander went, he developed colonies under Greek leadership. He developed trade and local governments. The Greek language became the second language for many diverse peoples. By the time the apostles went forth to preach the gospel, some four centuries later, Greek was spoken all around the Mediterranean. It was even the trade language of the Romans. In the marketplaces, on the docks, in the inns, everywhere, Greek was the people's language.

This common Greek is a very rich language in its background and diversity. A great body of literature has been found, including even letters and grocery bills, aiding us greatly in understanding terminology in the New Testament. This language also is quite easy to translate into English and other languages as well.

To maintain the flavor of this common Greek, it is generally better to translate it into the more common, everyday vocabulary of our own language than to adopt a lofty, literary mode. Jesus spoke to the common people, and they heard Him gladly. The apostles preached His gospel to people all over their world in this common Greek tongue. Most of the New Testament reflects the way people actually talked in those days. Alexander's influence lives on.

CHAPTER TWO

DAILY LIFE

What a novel idea! A theology that actually works! George was a teacher who took a prophetic posture in all that he taught. That is, the Christian faith must be a lived faith. For him, there must be clear and distinct ways in which what we say we believe comes out in practical, daily experience. The reflections that appear in this section pay tribute to one of George's most basic claims—namely, that unless our affirmation of faith shows up in concrete life, it has little credibility. For George, without a "rubber meets the road" quality to it, Christianity could not succeed.

By daily life, George does not mean merely living in the moment. According to George, simply living in the now degenerates into an escapist philosophy of life if it does not account for the responsibilities of adult living. The life of a Christian incorporates the importance of trusting God for our daily needs, balanced with developing a stewardship of talents God expects us to use for the advancement of the Kingdom. George emphasizes the importance of living for Christ today while appropriately planning for the future. This is simple living because it is focused on two things rather than thousands.

An aspect of daily life to which George draws our attention is the life of simplicity. For him, an overcomplicated life is a dissipated life. There is great satisfaction in choosing to live simply rather than frittering away our lives in useless detail. For example, instead of acquiring the many gadgets of a complicated life (items our culture says we must have), George prescribes that we find fulfillment and joy in living so as to make homes rather than houses.

Life is certainly more complicated at the end of the millennium than when George wrote about this challenge in 1977. He was cognizant that our culture was becoming addicted to complexity at the expense of simple daily living. The price of a complex life was too high for

George. The prophetic tone of his admonition to live simply is more relevant than when George first wrote it.

A Sense of Wonder

June 25, 1972

One day a number of years ago I stood at the rim of Crater Lake in Oregon marveling at the beauty of this mountain jewel. As I stood there a large black limousine stopped, a fur-coated lady got out with some others and approached the rim of the lake. She took one quick glance at the lake, turned on her heel and curtly said, "Well, we've seen it. Let's go."

What is it that so deadens the sense of wonder? Is it that we have marveled so often at the new things done by modern technology that we lose our ability to marvel anymore? Is it that men are so attached to material possessions that they cannot stop long enough to breathe the pine-scented air of the mountains or rest the eyes on the beauty of a deep-blue alpine lake? Probably there are all kinds of reasons, explanations, and guesses concerning this loss of wonder, but I believe that back of all of our interpretations there is really only one reason.

Men lose the capacity to wonder as they lose their sense of the reality of God. Often we quote from Psalm 19, "The heavens are telling of the glory of God; and the firmament is declaring the work of His hands" (v. 1, NAS). But men do not know God from nature. Men know nature from knowing God. The psalmist knew God, therefore the heavens showed God's glory to him. The heavens can't tell us who God is. God does that through His word and in Jesus. Once we know Him, then we marvel at His works.

David says it this way in Psalm 65, "Thou dost visit the earth, and cause it to overflow; Thou does greatly enrich it; the stream of God is full of water; Thou dost prepare their grain, for thus Thou dost prepare the earth" (v. 9, NAS). Appreciation of the beauty of the earth is ours when we appreciate the Creator. Failing to know Him, we live, like that woman at Crater Lake, with the sense of wonder stilled.

Are Drunks Really Funny?

October 14, 1973

Comedians have a field day caricaturing drunks. If the performers do it well, audiences laugh hilariously. People laugh when they see a man who can't walk straight, talk straight, maintain a straight line of thought, or control his emotions. How funny is that, really? We'd feel deeply offended to see a comedian caricaturing a man in a wheelchair or a person sick with palsy. One set of disabilities is brought about by forces beyond oneself, the other by the choice to drink. Neither is funny.

When we consider the cost in human misery, drunkenness becomes a matter for tears, not for laughter. The California Highway Patrol Commissioner, Walter Pudinski, reports that fifty percent of fatal traffic accidents involve drunken drivers. He estimates that there will be 115,000 arrests in California in 1973 for drunken driving. In the ten years we were involved in the war in Vietnam 55,000 Americans were killed. In the United States during that same period 500,000 Americans were killed in traffic accidents! Drunks were involved in a large percentage of those fatalities. That's not funny.

But the human misery surfaces only partially in auto wrecks. Think of the broken homes, the children who live with drunken, quarreling adults, the broken bodies of men and women destroyed by alcohol, and the loss to society of both the alcoholic's contribution and the time used by many others in attempts to help him or assume his responsibility. None of that is funny.

Deeper still, how can it be funny that a human being, made in the image of God, declared by God to be a little lower than the angels, should set aside his dignity and value as God's creation to be destroyed by liquor?

When we consider even briefly the enormity of the drinking problem in our society, the drunk either real or caricatured should bring us to weep, not to laugh. A man destroyed by alcohol isn't funny.

Only One Day?

May 19, 1974

"Live just one day at a time" is advice commonly given to people who seem too anxious about the problems of the future. In a way this is good advice. A lot of worrying concerns things we can't change anyway, and in many cases we worry about things that never happen at all. So it is a good idea to live each day for the values and opportunities in that day, not borrowing from the uncertain future.

But "Live just one day at a time" can be pretty bad advice under some circumstances, and it might be a downright escapist philosophy as well. It's true that birds don't worry about the future, but they do nest, migrate, and make other suitable adjustments for survival. And ants are industrious enough to prepare for days to come. We are more suitably prepared than birds or ants to know about the future and to plan and prepare for it. On the philosophy of "just one day at a time" one could get into debt that he could never repay, pass by the best years for a college education, and refuse to develop talents because on any individual day these talents seem so untrained.

"One day at a time" can be a way to refuse adult responsibilities. How may children are born to people who lived only for the moment and who never contemplated the dedication to the future required by those who bring new life into this world?

Jesus taught us not to be anxious for the morrow, but He also taught us how foolish it is for a man to start things without counting the cost. A Christian who lives in constant anxiety has not learned to trust Him who cares for us. A Christian who refuses to be concerned with any day but the present will fail in his stewardship of talents and potentials which God has granted him.

Generation Language

November 10, 1974

Every generation has its own language. This language is more than just the words that are spoken. It involves modes of dress, possessions, personal grooming, music, humor, and political and religious expression. Part of this distinctive generation language comes about just because times change; part of it is deliberately contrived to emphasize difference. Young people are always the new generation. They want that to be known. In one sense they are forced into that distinction, and in another sense they choose that distinction. They are young and there is nothing they can do about that. They can emphasize this distinction if they wish and they usually seem to want to do this.

When adults try to overcome the "generation gap" by attempting to copy youth's generation language the situations often are ludicrous. A balding, fifty-year-old man with a wisp of long hair waving down his back or a stout, miniskirted grandmother just doesn't impress anyone as genuine. They just can't speak the generation language of youth. The gap between kids and adults isn't overcome this way. Nor is it overcome by adults trying to force young people to adopt the language of adults in dress, music, hair style, and the like.

The difference between generations is inevitable, and it is needed. Young people need an identity with their own age groups, and they need also the stability of adults who are adults and who do not violate that role in a vain attempt to bridge the gap. Children need parents to be parents. No one else can do this. They don't want their parents to be children, brothers and sisters, or buddies—just parents. The language of personal integrity is understood and appreciated everywhere.

Why Solitude?

July 6, 1975

Here in my study I have a picture of John Muir taken when he was twenty-three. Beneath that picture is this quote from him: "Everybody needs Beauty as well as bread, places to pray in and play in, where Nature may heal and cheer and give strength to body and soul alike." Throughout his lifetime Muir enjoyed a great amount of solitude and he felt that others needed solitude also.

Why solitude? Most of our time is spent in cooperative enterprises. We are subjected to massive media communication which almost constantly imposes upon us books, billboards, radio, television, magazines, and newspapers. And, although to some degree we can turn these off or turn from them, the pressure and habits of life draw us to them as insects are drawn to light.

As long as we find meaning only in this communal way we lack in the understanding of self, of God, and of others that solitude can bring. Prophets have always known that a clear vision of the world and its affairs comes when one climbs the heights of solitude. A few days ago a dear friend of mine went away for several days to sort things out. My friend returned with a clearer vision of self and a profoundly improved sense of other relationships.

Summer is vacation time for millions of people. Do you plan to arrange some time for solitude? Will all your time vacationing just be a more intense involvement with more people and problems? In the midst of service and busyness Jesus called the disciples away for solitude. In solitude we see more clearly what God wants us to be and what He wants us to do. A few days in solitude can help us arrange life's priorities and so increase the joy and fruitfulness of many other days.

Honest Behavior

November 14, 1976

We've heard a lot about truth and honesty lately. We ought to hear a lot about it. It's an important subject, so important that Jesus said we should mean "yes" and "no" when we say those words. But we have a tendency to confine honesty to statements of fact or intent, such as reports of what we did or said or heard or will do. What about honest behavior?

By honest behavior I mean the kind of action that is consistent with our awareness of ourselves and reality around us. Just as we expect honest words to conform to facts, so we should expect honest actions to conform to honest awareness. Why not sleep when sleep is a felt need? Why should dad, driving the car, refuse to admit sleepiness until an accident proves he was sleepy? Why, when the appetite is satisfied, should we eat more to please a hostess or so that the food will not be wasted?

"Yes" and "no" apply in many situations. A friend makes a sharp, critical, but funny remark about you or someone else. Honest action is to respond, "I'm hurt by that," or "I don't feel right to have you say that about Harry." Dishonest action is silence, agreement, laughter.

Suddenly the overwhelming impulse to reach out and hug a son or daughter and express warmth and love comes upon us. But we hold back because we don't want them to see and feel our emotion. That's dishonest action. Or we make a great fuss about approving the actions of someone who can benefit us, even though we do not approve those actions. That's dishonest action.

"Let your yes be yes and your no be no" goes beyond words.

You Don't Buy a Home

March 27, 1977

Many of us have contracts on houses. Ours is for thirty years. After 360 payments the house belongs to us. But we don't buy a home when we buy a house. We make a home, and that can be done without a house. A house is just a building; a home is living, relationships, work, joy, tears—a lot of things.

Edgar Guest captured the idea when he said: "It takes a heap of living in a house to make it home." Someone else said that it is "something you've been through with someone."

This is why people get frustrated when they extend themselves financially for good furniture, drapes, carpets and decorations and then find that they are no happier than before. I've even seen parents pressure the children to protect the furniture as if the material things were more important than the children. I remember one mother who used to lock her children out of the house when she left to go shopping so that they wouldn't mess things up.

Since we don't buy homes, we can start anytime to make one. A young couple in Oregon made a home in a one-room cabin built of unpainted, rough-sawed lumber. Their possessions were few and very simple, but they had a home because they built that simple cabin into one: they loved the Lord and they loved each other.

At their table I drank water from a pint-size jar. It was good water. And the real thrill was that they didn't apologize for not having real water glasses. Those jars worked just fine. That couple was thankful for what they had. They had a home.

Many times I've tried to help people who had expensive houses. People who had no homes. That's sad—to have everything and not to have a home. I'm thankful that I grew up in a poor family, living in pretty humble houses, but we always had a home.

Much of modern alienation, loneliness and despair comes about because people just live in houses.

The old house will fall down. Let's build homes. They'll last.

You Choose Simplicity

May 8, 1977

Thoreau put it this way: "Simplicity, simplicity, simplicity! I say let your affairs be as two or three, and not a hundred or a thousand." You choose simplicity; complication seeks you out. We live in a world of detail. Without a conscious effort toward simplicity, we get so caught up in the details that we become slaves to much that is of no importance at all.

We buy a bewildering array of gadgets, most of them hooked to electricity to do things faster with more energy consumption, and, supposedly, to free our precious time. But we must work to pay for that energy. Maybe just opening the cans with a simple, manual can opener would save us time in the long run.

We use; we discard. That's the very hallmark of our affluent society, and it's more complicated that way than to have things that last.

In my first backpack trips into the mountains years ago, I worked for a variety in meals that exceeded what I had at home. Then it dawned on me that I was needlessly complicating my affairs when what I really wanted was simplicity. So I found a few satisfying foods that could be used in a few different combinations, and now I have no hassle in getting ready to go. Furthermore, I have more real freedom in the outdoors than I had known before.

We can get so caught up in reading every new thing that we never read any book thoroughly, or delight in what a writer says if we knew him as a friend. Speed-reading with all its virtues may often be just another device at endless complication.

Every manufacturer and every promoter has his agenda for making life more confused. A deliberate choice is essential if we really want simplicity. This life-style runs against the grain of our culture. But that choice for simplicity is like the choice to turn the handle tight on a dripping faucet. It keeps us from frittering away our interest, our money, and our efforts in useless detail. The satisfaction from simplicity is great gain.

They Never Really Closed the Colosseum

July 24, 1977

I was both impressed and depressed when I visited the Colosseum in Rome. Opened in 79 A.D. by Vespasian, the Colosseum could seat between forty and fifty thousand people. It stood 160 feet high and enclosed an area about the size of a football field. The name "Colosseum" was derived from a large statue (Colossus) of Nero at the entrance by Hadrian.

Standing in the ruins of this great monument from the past, I was impressed with its size, that it has survived centuries of use as a stone quarry for building many other buildings, and that it stands as a reminder of the engineering and building skills of people now gone from the earth almost two thousand years.

But I was depressed, too. I managed to visit early one morning when only a few people were around. It was quiet in the great inner cavern of that amphitheatre. I imagined the crowds and began to hear the screams of pain from dying animals and men and women who suffered there for the satisfaction of the mobs.

Over five thousand animals died there in just the opening dedication ceremonies. On a given day four hundred bears were put to death. Rare animals were hunted down and captured to bring to this place to die in terrible ways before the jeering crowds. And Christians died here for their faith in Jesus. In the quiet of my morning there I grew inwardly sick and depressed with sinful man's inhumanity and depravity.

Is it really closed? Do we attend the auto race for the disastrous wreck? Do we feel no offense at the bloodletting in boxing? Why are great young athletes destroyed on football fields? How many people go forth with high powered weapons, hunting the satisfaction of conquest in the death of an animal? And the violence in TV and motion pictures tells us that the Colosseum is still open. Time doesn't remove the Colosseum and its cruel violence. Conversion to Christ does that. That's the only way it will ever really be closed.

Computer Mentality

March 30, 1980

Computers work on the binary system. Electric circuits are either on or off, or plus or minus, so that a computer has no gray area of part way on or part way off. A computer has a black-or-white mentality.

We can also get caught up in this computer way of looking at things. We may discover that carbon-14 administered to animals in heavy concentrations will induce cancer and then panic over even the most minor of dosages. Yet most of what we eat has some carbon-14 in it, and we can't stop eating. Likewise, water has come deuterium in it, and deuterium could be lethal in sufficiently heavy concentrations. But we can't stop drinking water. It has been pointed out that if aspirin were not already cleared for production and distribution, it would be exceedingly difficult today to get it by our maze of regulatory agencies.

Now I am not contending that the enemy of all progress is regulation. But computer thinking gets us into the habit of thinking in absolutes; we find it hard to recognize that we are not absolutely endangered by everything that would wipe us out if the dosage were large enough. It just isn't true that because sugar can be destructive to tooth enamel that no sugar should be eaten. And it is not true that if, because of human need, we happen to displace or even destroy some plant or animal that the whole universe of life will disintegrate.

Life just isn't this simple. Everything is not played out in absolute rights and wrongs. It is vital for us to understand this in our modern technological age. We must accept some curses along with the blessings. Disappointments come because we so often look upon each scientific advance as an absolute solution.

Antibiotics were supposed to wipe out disease, the atom to provide boundless energy, and the green revolution to eliminate hunger. So what happens? We get some diseases curbed and others come to the front. The atom gives us energy but also a source of pollution. More food and more medicine increase population and bring hunger again to more people than were ever hungry before.

Computer thinking wants everything to be either right or wrong. The reality is that we have to live with these stresses because we have no absolutely perfect solutions. It's important that we have enough humility to give some room for the grays. Otherwise, we may very well find ourselves lining up on every issue with such inflexible positions that we cannot find even partially right solutions.

Hearing the Corn Grow

November 30, 1980

In tall corn country, people often say that they can hear the corn grow. I'm not sure that I have ever actually heard corn grow, but in good, warm growing weather one can recognize with each new day that the corn is taller. Of course, we don't expect it to get shorter. Corn grows. That's its nature. That's the nature of all living things. It is this process of dependable growth that encourages the farmer. He has faith in the process. His livelihood depends upon it. In fact, we all depend upon it.

All my life, it seems, I have been growing plants. Reared on a farm, I have never departed from my rural connections and have always gardened and eaten from the fruits of this labor. In other ways, as well, I have enjoyed the growth process. Teaching Greek for twenty-five years in San Jose Bible College, I watched this process of growth in my students as they moved from a few oral Greek words to the alphabet, then to simple sentences, and on to the complexities of the language of the New Testament. Language teaching and learning provides teacher and students with definite goals, predictable accomplishments, and a constant sense of achievement.

Just desire alone will not bring a student to a reading knowledge of Greek. A great musician is born with talent, but disciplined practice is essential to the development of that talent. Any complex performance is based upon many hours of practice.

Growth in the knowledge of our Lord Jesus Christ is a process too. No one is born into the kingdom in full strength and maturity. Growth should be perceptible. From year to year we should be able to mark our Christian development in those qualities of the spirit that define the nature of His people.

The world around us realizes the vital, living presence of Christ in the growing, maturing personalities of Christians. It is a real testimony to His power when others see and hear Christians grow!

"Only Forgiven"?

December 14, 1980

Have you seen the bumper sticker that reads "Christians aren't perfect, only forgiven"? I'm bothered by the implication of that motto. Surely, who of us would deny the words alone? Absolute perfection is obviously not ours in our own strength or practice. It is God's grace that includes us in His family, not human perfection.

But on a bumper sticker, does this declaration offer an excuse for bad driving? Is this a cover statement for exceeding the speed limit, arrogance in passing and lane changing, or rolling stops at stop signs? Does such a bumper sticker say "Since I'm a forgiven Christian I don't need to take traffic laws very seriously"? Does it say "Don't expect any special courtesy from me; I goof up a lot when I drive"?

When I see a car with the fish symbol in the window, or with a bumper sticker displaying a Scripture phrase, or with "Warning, At the Rapture This Car Will Be Driverless," I'm inclined to expect conformity to law, courtesy, and general good manners. If I don't see these things I wonder what kind of Christian is at the wheel.

And what happened to "Be ye perfect as your heavenly Father is perfect"? Are we afraid of that? Sure, that statement alone, without Scriptural context, can also be misunderstood. But it does urge an ideal that we cannot easily set aside in our practice. Let's face it—we always run a risk when we try to share our faith in simplistic ways.

Bumper sticker theology is not confined to bumper stickers. It can crop up in many different ways. We had better be sensitive to how we try to share the gospel so that we do not unwittingly distort the message that the world receives from us. It is a fact; we aren't perfect theologians, just trying.

To a Hummingbird

July 5, 1981

Today I held a hummingbird in my hands—tiny, vibrant with life, and so frightened.

His wings had whirred and his tiny body had battered the glass. Beyond the glass was freedom, the whole outdoors. Yet he was captured. The door behind him was wide open, big enough for a car. He'd come in that way. But he did not see the door. Even my efforts to redirect his flight led only to more frantic struggle for escape. He was beating out his energy in an impossible quest, trapped by his limited perception. He could never break through that glass.

I reached out and covered him gently in the darkness of my cupped hands. He didn't make a move, just rested there in the darkness and warmth as I carried him through the big door into the open. I opened my hands, and he soared away, almost straight up high above me, into the top of a stately fir tree.

How many times my frantic pursuit of life, of freedom, of hope has found me beating out my energy in vain human efforts to achieve. In calm submission to His covering hands I find a quiet place. In His warm, tender, loving hands my mind cools, my spirit finds peace, and in this stillness He releases me to the freedom that He alone can give.

Tiny bird, in my hands could you feel my love? I will never know; you are a mystery to me. But you have a part in His care. You cannot fall without Him knowing.

I touched you today; you touched me, too. In those brief moments our lives met. You found life again, your freedom. And you carried a message to me: my life is in His care. It was His larger hands today that touched us both.

Are You Eating Out Today?

August 9, 1981

Not long ago, I was eating out with friends after morning worship where I had been the guest speaker. And I got to wondering, "What if?" "What if Christians didn't eat out on Sundays?"

Many restaurants get flooded with customers right after the churches let out on Sunday morning, and many have a lot of business after evening service, too. So Sunday business would be down if the church crowd just didn't show up.

And if Christians didn't eat out on Sundays, I'm sure some of the people who cook, clean, and serve would be free from Sunday work. There would be some Christians free to attend services and to participate more fully in congregational life if businesses were not open on Sundays.

And if Christians didn't eat out on Sundays, we wouldn't be saying to the world that it is ok to work on Sundays and keep businesses open. The Bible-packing, sermon-reviewing crowd wouldn't be telling waitresses, "We've had a busy two hours serving the Lord, and we're here now for you to serve us."

And if Christians didn't eat out on Sundays then we'd be eating in our homes; maybe we'd even get together more and share our food and our time with each other. Maybe we'd spontaneously organize some potlucks or have sandwich and soup get-togethers.

We have kitchens, dishes, food, and dining rooms, but we pay others to cook for us and serve us. Why?

I haven't found one good reason yet for eating out on Sundays. Good reasons for not doing this are easier to come by. If we didn't eat out, wouldn't it be a great witness to the world? We wouldn't be asking others to serve us on the day when everyone ought to share fellowship in church meetings. And we'd get rid of the gnawing guilt that comes as we patronize the seven-day business week.

Have we gotten caught up in a self-indulgent, luxury habit with this out-on-Sunday eating? Are we saying what we really want to say to others about Christian living?

Solitude

November 28, 1982

Everyone needs some quiet times, moments of reflection and solitude in which to gather things together and to sort things out. Such moments may be snatched out of the fires of busyness, planned in special ways, or just come to us as the accidents of timing.

Usually we must plan to have moments for solitude. The times when we feel we can least afford quietness and prayer are the very times we need most to put our priority there.

Jesus counseled us to pray in secret; then the Father who hears and sees in secret will respond to us and to our needs. It isn't that praying in public is bad, unless we pray to be seen praying. It's just that there are qualities of solitude with God that cannot be had in any other way than to go to the secret place.

Just the contrast of the quiet moments with the racket and confusion in much of modern life can be refreshing. I like early-morning country walks. There's not much besides severe weather or poor health that can prevent these walks for me. I can't go as frequently as I would like to the high mountains, but I can walk in the country in the morning. These are my times of creative silence. With His great nature paintings before me and His creatures along the roads and trails and flying overhead, my inner thoughts naturally turn to the Creator, the Covenant Maker, our Heavenly Father. Thoughts that may lie buried in the busyness of life come to bloom in the solitude of prayer and meditation.

But solitude without the sense of His presence may simply degenerate the mind and deaden the soul. Sigurd Olson tells of an old recluse in Alaska who read only the Bible for years and was always anxious to talk about it with anyone who came by. He had bitterly concluded, however, that "the Bible is a pack of lies." He had missed the Author. In his outdoor habitat he'd never seen the hand of the Creator. What a waste! He had traveled along the old, quiet, primitive road to find some meaning for his life and had failed.

Physical meals are essential for our physical health. Spiritual meals are equally essential for our spiritual health. The inner life finds strength in solitude.

Beware of Constant Approval

July 15, 1984

"Woe to you when all men speak well of you, for in the same way their fathers used to treat the false prophets" (Luke 6:26, *New American Standard Bible*). Politics is the science of popularity. Politics employs strategies for gaining approval. That's going on all around us right now in this election summer of 1984.

Of course, we expect this to be true in a free country like ours where leaders are chosen by ballots, not by bullets. But why is Jesus critical of this strategy of gaining approval? He pronounces a woe on us when we are approved by everybody. What's wrong with fitting in everywhere?

Maybe that's it. If we fit in everywhere and we are constantly accepted by others in all circumstances, we just have to be adjusting daily to the winds of change. A contemporary of Socrates said that he hated Socrates because he made him face the truth about himself. And this is why Christians cannot fit in everywhere. The Christian way, the life-style of the reborn, stands out in stark contrast to that of many of the unsaved. Peter says that the people of this world are "surprised that you do not run with them in the same excess of dissipation, and they malign you" (1 Peter 4:4, *New American Standard Bible*).

It's not at all difficult to become involved in accommodating this world's ungodly views because of the desire we have to fit in and not make waves. We may quiescently assent to the crimes of public officials, accepting the generalized and untrue doctrine that the commonality of guilt mitigates evil. "All politicians are like that" seems the end of the matter. "Oh, sure, I don't obey the speed laws, but who does? I'd be run over if I did."

We can also get caught up by the talk-show passion for association with unsavory persons as long as they are successful, well-known, and generally approved by the standards of the day. And how easily we can be tempted to betray confidences, to become a special information source for others in a group of gossips and slanderers. We can't get the words back once we've spoken them.

In so many ways, our desire to be accepted leads us into conduct that does not fit the Christian pattern. The Pharisees were condemned by Jesus for seeking the approval of men more than the approval of God. That temptation is always present in this world that places high value on social adaptation.

Times have not changed. The trap is still baited. Woe to us when we take that bait! We had better pay attention to what Jesus said. We may be on the wrong road, the broad way, if we are accepted and approved by everyone everywhere.

The Magic of the Custom

May 5, 1985

For some years I taught public speaking at a large university of about twenty-five thousand students. Every semester each new class came to the first session quite apprehensive. The students didn't know me, nor did they know one another, and they *did* know that they were going to have to make "speeches." I tried a number of procedures in attempts to put them at ease and to get them acquainted with me and with each other.

After several years of only passable success, an old idea came to mind. The more I thought about this old idea, the more it seemed to me that it would be startlingly new in this university context. So I decided to try it at the initial meeting of my new Tuesday evening class.

I went to the classroom early and arranged the chairs in a semicircular pattern in front of my teaching desk. Then I propped the door open and took my position beside the door in the hallway outside my classroom. Generally, the more timid, more apprehensive students arrive first, particularly at the first class session. They like to get situated well toward the back of the room, trying to be unnoticed. Soon I sighted my first student. She was coming down the long hallway rather tentatively, reading room numbers along the way. She saw the number about my door and hesitantly approached.

"Hello," I greeted her. "I'm Mr. Alder. You're looking for Speech 20A, I hope." I extended my hand and she extended hers. We shook hands.

"I'm Debbie Carstens. Yes, I'm looking for Speech 20A, and my card says that you are my teacher."

"Glad to have you in class, Debbie. Where are you from?"

And so it went, students coming, shaking hands, giving me names and other information and then entering the room. Finally, I entered the room, closed the door, and sat on the edge of my desk. My students were engaged in animated conversations; the whole room just buzzed with talk. At last I interrupted. "Class, class, I'm sorry that I have to intrude on your visits. I know you are having a good time getting acquainted. I hate to stop this, but there are several things that I'm kind of obligated to take care of at this first session. Please bear with me for a little while."

Friendly greetings and handshakes had changed everything. Something we do in church all the time was just as effective, maybe more so, in this university setting in relieving tensions and starting communication.

What does this mean? Human warmth and friendliness are never out of style. We are all looking for people who are open to us, willing to talk with us, and willing to accept us as equals.

The friendly greeting and handshakes given by thousands and received by thousands in the entryways of churches every Sunday probably account for more people beginning their journey to Jesus than any other simple thing we do. There is a kind of magic in this old custom.

CHAPTER THREE
THE CHURCH

George Alder was passionate about Church. From his boyhood in Washington through his college days in Eugene, Oregon, serving God through the Church became a major priority. He once participated in some debates over how Scripture should be interpreted with regard to worship and musical instruments. He was deeply concerned over how the Church should respond to modern culture and issues arising in the 60's and 70's. His intimate acquaintance with original Greek language allowed him to comment on Church concerns with unique perspective and compelling incisive logic. Coming from the Stone-Campbell movement, which is a unity and restoration movement, you will note columns aimed at those subjects. The articles chosen for this section display the breadth and scope of his concerns—enough to make most of us alternatively glad and mad. His was not just a West Coast or American concern. Always concerned about the larger world, he and Eileen traveled around the world expressing solidarity with the Church, buttressed by a lifetime of prayer and financial support of Church and missionary activity.

Would Jesus Go to Church?

January 2, 1972

Churchgoing isn't nearly as popular now as it has been in some periods. No community pressure is exerted on people to force attendance, and a lot of church members demonstrate little persistence or consistency in attendance. Many confess to a feeling of boredom and irrelevance in the church services. Some contend that the whole thing smacks too much of tradition, a kind of retreat into the mythical stability of a bygone world. And then the question is raised, "Would Jesus go to church?" Usually, when that question is asked it is asked in a context implying that Jesus wouldn't go to church.

How can anyone be that sure? True, He did blast the religious leaders of His day because they were hung up in traditions. They honored traditions, but forgot love, mercy, and justice. But Jesus never advocated that people forsake the law, refuse to make sacrifices, stay away from the festivals or picket the synagogues. "He went," we are told, "as his custom was to the synagogue."

I believe that Jesus would go to church, and I believe He is in His church. He is the head of the body. The church is more than a building—it is the people gathered in faith and commitment to Him. He said that the day would come when neither in Jerusalem nor in Samaria, on particular mountains, would men gather to worship, but in spirit and truth.

When we ask, "Would He go to church?" we are really asking whether He would support much of what we call church today. He'd embarrass us about questions of tradition and religious ritual as He discomfited the Pharisees in Palestine. He died for the church. We aren't following Him when we refuse to share in that body. He promised to be with His people, so assuredly He goes to church!

Must We Sing?

June 3, 1973

Have you ever felt put upon by a songleader who urges, "Let's sing like we meant it," or "Come on now, I know you can sing louder than that," or "Smile, when you sing: be happy"? Maybe we've felt like the people Malachi talks about who complained of worship, "What a weariness it is." When our mood is wrong we feel like everything else should reflect our feelings; we object to urgings to cheer up and be happy.

But how meaningful is our singing anyway? I discovered recently that I take congregational singing for granted. One Sunday I went to church unable to sing because of laryngitis. I read the songs. I felt uncomfortable not being able to share. What was bothering me? I tried to analyze this. Gradually I realized what was wrong. Singing together is a wonderful expression of corporate faith and aspiration. Praising God with other Christians is a lifting, vital fellowship. I was missing this.

How great it was to hear those wonderful hymns, "Come Thou Almighty King," "My Jesus I Love Thee," and "Beneath the Cross of Jesus." When the invitation was sung, a mother and father and five daughters responded. Mother and Dad and two daughters came to unite with us in fellowship; the three younger daughters confessed faith in Jesus.

Before these lovely girls were baptized, the congregation sang "Anywhere with Jesus," "Wonderful Words of Life," and "Take My Life and Let It Be." As each person came up from the water, the choir led the congregation in responding "Now She Belongs to Jesus." I wanted to sing, too. Amidst tears of joy I recognized how important worship is to me.

Maybe we do exhort one another to sing with rather poor motivational devices. Maybe at times it's all too slow, or too fast, or too loud or too soft. But just being prevented from sharing can remind us powerfully that this fellowship is important. We are not isolated Christians. Jesus saved us into His body. Now I understand better why we are called upon to "be filled with the Spirit; speaking to yourselves in psalms and hymns and spiritual songs, singing and making melody in your heart to the Lord" (Ephesians 5:18, 19).

Not Forsaking the Assembling

June 9, 1974

Modern electronic technology in sound reproduction makes it possible for us to hear music in our living rooms with a fidelity that rivals the concert hall. In fact, sometimes the sound may even be better than it would have been in some of the far corners of the great hall. I've found great enjoyment in music because of these tremendous advances in high-fidelity stereo systems.

However, the experience of hearing the music of the chamber group, the symphony, or the opera in one's living room is not the same as hearing it in the concert hall or opera house. Why, what's different? We aren't involved with people in the same way. There is something about going out in the evening to join with the others of common interest, to feel the responses of the group toward the artists and the music and actually to see the music being made that is just not present when we listen at home.

Corporate worship is a lot like this. Surely we can read the Bible at home, sing at home, pray at home; but this is not the same as it is when we join with the family of God in sharing together. If there is some spirit of commonality and aesthetic enjoyment in the concert hall, then surely in worship there is a greater spirit because that which draws us together goes far beyond human genius and artistry.

Have you ever had to eat your meals alone for any extended period? That's really a dreary experience for most of us because mealtime is more than just feeding the body. The sense of fellowship at the table transcends the actual physical need.

Worship with God's people transcends all our physical needs and enhances all of life with a sense of His presence and a confidence and security in His body that separatistic worship cannot bring. I believe that is why there is so much emphasis in the Bible on worshipping God with all the saints. Maybe the reason I enjoy music reproduced in my home is just because I've also enjoyed it over and over again with other music lovers in the concert hall.

Similarly, my personal devotion is meaningful because I am a member of His body and I worship every week with the family of God.

What's a Campbellite?

January 26, 1975

If you don't know what a Campbellite is or was then somewhere along the line you've either forgotten or you've never known it at all. Why is it even important to know this? It's important just in the same way that many other historical facts are important. History, our connection with the past, provides a basis for coping with the present and with the future. "Campbellite" is a term out of our past, and whether we know this term or not says something about what we know of the religious movement of which we are the heirs and, hopefully, the proponents.

Thomas Campbell and his son, Alexander, were prime movers during the first half of the nineteenth century for non-denominational, New Testament Christianity. In a time when bitter religious division and exaggerated denominational loyalty severed believer from believer, these men and others urged a return to the Bible as the sole basis for faith and Christian living. They argued that creedal statements in addition to the Bible which either added to or subtracted from the teachings of Scripture were the cause of strife and division. They urged a return to what Jesus and His apostles had taught on salvation, the church, the Christian life, and all other pertinent doctrines.

They were bitterly assailed by denominational leaders, yet their appeal struck home with multitudes, making this the fastest growing religious movement in America. Holding the followers of this simple Biblical Christianity up to scorn, their enemies called them "Campbellites." In this way they tried to associate this powerfully influential teaching with men and separate it from the Bible.

Name calling is often resorted to by those who cannot meet the truth. This is what happened then. So "Campbellite," meant to be a term of derision, actually embodies much in our history to honor. Certainly we don't want to be known as followers of men, but we can honor those who in our history taught us to leave men to follow the Bible.

Indigenous Is Not Only for the Mission Fields

October 19, 1975

I've been hearing missionaries tell how the concept of the indigenous church has changed missionary methods and stimulated church growth fantastically. The idea is simple. People in all countries can become Christians and they can understand the Scriptures and be the body of Christ without foreign domination. This means that American missionaries do not try to Americanize people in India, Africa, or other countries, but simply Christianize them with the gospel.

This has meant the end of foreign domination, the mission compound, and that attitude of superiority that often stood as a barrier to those who did not know Jesus.

We generally applaud this change and express confidence that the gospel is not an American invention and that it certainly transcends all cultures and is not first concerned with food, clothing, music, organization, and other things that differ in various cultures.

Great! But are we as willing to see that the concept of the indigenous church is just as valid in our own country? Must churches in California insist that churches in Indiana and Illinois, or in Texas and Oklahoma, follow the patterns that seem to be appropriate in California? And must Christians in other sections of the USA insist that Christians in California or Texas conform to all the cultural likes and dislikes of other sections of the country?

We have great cultural variety across this nation. Sometimes within a short distance, even within a city, such variety is obvious. One group of Christians may prefer a church with vaulted roof, a great organ, and a very formal service. Others in the same city may prefer a community hall approach with drums and guitars. Why judge each other? If the church is really indigenous, then that should be true at home as well as on mission fields.

Declarations for Unity

July 4, 1976

While politics heats up in 1976 we may indulge the illusion that it was on the basis of a great national unity that the colonies declared independence two hundred years ago. As a matter of fact, perhaps a third of the Americans would have preferred to retain membership in the British Empire. Somewhere near fifty thousand of these "Loyalists" fought with the British against the "Patriots." Often Washington's forces were so surrounded by Loyalists that he was at the disadvantage of fighting in enemy territory.

Although the dream of a union has been accomplished, the dream of a genuine unity is very hard to achieve. The very nature of our country has meant proliferation of ideas in politics, in religion, in economics, in just about everything. We inherit a tradition of disagreement. And we also inherit the American conviction that everyone should have the right to speak his mind.

Following the two wars with Britain, an American religious movement gained momentum. This movement distinguished itself by the call for unity of diverse religious parties. Thomas Campbell brought the concept of this restoration movement into focus in his Declaration and Address. Simply stated, he argued for unity in Christ based upon acceptance of Him as given in Scripture. The old creed books of denominational separation were to be cast aside in favor of the Bible alone. As Luther had three centuries earlier asked for a return to Scripture, so the restorationists asked for a fulfillment of that Reformation.

Two great dreams that New Testament Christians in America have inherited from the past need expression in our country and in the world now. Society torn by economic, religious, political, and social strife needs the unifying concept of our Declaration of Independence and Constitution and the powerful divine direction of God's Word as promoted in the Declaration and Address.

Great truths are more than national in application; they belong to all people. The world needs the unifying power of these two declarations. Without them we move toward chaos.

He Couldn't Practice It

April 3, 1977

In 1829 Alexander Campbell debated the industrialist-philanthropist Robert Owen on the evidences of Christianity. Owen claimed that all the misery in the world came from three things: private property, indissoluble marriage and religion. He did not believe the Bible; he read it when he was twelve years old and decided it wasn't true!

Owen's thinking appears to have influenced Karl Marx. So we can see that in debating Owen, Alexander Campbell was defending the Bible against the rising rationalistic humanism and communism that characterizes our century. In this sense, this debate was *the* debate of the nineteenth century, more important than the famous Lincoln-Douglas debates in terms of the ultimate issues at stake.

But Owen couldn't practice his own convictions. He was a man of private property. He was very wealthy. His textile plants prospered and he was innovative in industry and in education. Although he saw indissoluble marriage as a hindrance to human happiness, he remained faithfully married throughout his life to his Christian wife. And although he said that religion produced human misery and that the revelation of the Bible was a pretension, he proposed "twelve laws" which he claimed were divinely given.

He tried to make his ideas work in a community called New Harmony. His commune failed as did many other such attempts by others throughout that century. The trouble was that he believed in the perfectability of human beings apart from God. No one has ever been able to build a perfect society with that kind of material. So Owen couldn't practice what he believed, because what he believed missed the mark of reality. Campbell set down the solid basis for a perfect social order—the Bible. What he taught can be practiced; it agrees with the divine order. Now we, the Lord's body, His church, must model that divine order in our assemblies and advocate and live it in our communities. The principles of the Christian religion are intended to be demonstrated in practice, because—unlike the principles of every humanistic world order—they work.

Fences Around Graveyards

November 11, 1979

Bishop Gerald Kennedy of the Methodist Church tells of a little town that got into a big problem over a five-hundred-thousand-dollar donation from a will. The money got into the hands of the cemetery board, and, among other things, they decided to build a fence around the cemetery. Then they became divided over what kind of fence to build, living roses or wrought iron. Eventually, the whole town was split over this issue and everyone was mad.

Kennedy was asked to come as a peacemaker to a town meeting. He totally failed to get the people together. Then a preacher from a little Pentecostal church spoke up. "Folks," he said, "as I see it, no one in the cemetery is going to get out, and no one outside wants to get in. So we don't need a fence. Let's build a playground for our kids." And that's what they did.

Kennedy concludes that too many churches are building fences around cemeteries. We get caught up with fencing-in dead issues, past and gone and buried, when we ought to be facing up to the challenges of the real world in which we now live. We often find it easier, and less risky, to build a fence around some old doctrinal distinction about musical instruments, or some other equally "important" issue, than to tackle the task of evangelizing the community where we live. There are a lot of people left dying along the Jerico Road while religious people are caught up in arguing about fences.

We need to free ourselves from this fence-building syndrome and start thinking about and praying about the unsaved, the starving, the imprisoned, and all the rest of those who are suffering—the people for whom Jesus died.

After all, if we did build a really good fence around a graveyard, what purpose would it serve?

"As Christ Received You"

June 8, 1980

It was our first visit to Mexico. The first Sunday of that visit we were guests in a little rural church. After I was introduced, I was immediately asked to serve at the Lord's table with one of the men of that congregation. He prayed in Spanish; I prayed in English. How marvelous to be accepted in this way! They received me just as Christ had received them.

They didn't ask how we worshipped in San Jose, California—whether we lifted our hands, stomped our feet, clapped our hands, shouted "Amens" or closed our eyes when we prayed. They didn't check my skin color, ask about my financial or political position, or even request an official church letter of introduction. These wonderful Christians received me without looking for points of difference or opportunities for dispute.

Where do we find the text to justify an attack on a brother because his church is too small or too large? What Scripture says that I know the motivation in your heart for buying a new car, giving an emotional testimony, singing in the choir, or weeping during the Communion? And who are you or who am I to criticize a minister for trying to get large crowds to attend services? Who ever gave us the right to judge God's servants?

Those dear brothers and sisters in that little congregation in Mexico didn't comment on the length of my hair, whether my tie and shirt matched, or what translation of the Bible I used. They accepted me. They didn't offer a theory of fellowship, a doctrine of Communion, rules for worship, or a final judgment on the ERA. They accepted me as Christ had accepted me, openly in trust and in love.

There are enough enemies outside the church. By the mercies of God let us within the church be brothers!

Shall Not All Serve?

March 8, 1981

There must be exceptions to the general practice that only men serve the Lord's Supper, but I seldom encounter them. Why is this? Why is it that it's always "The men will come forward to serve the Lord's Supper"? There isn't any New Testament teaching that sets such a restriction. Why should we limit such service to adult male members of the congregation? In some congregations this service is restricted to elected elders and deacons only.

Since the Lord's Supper is a gathering of the family of God around the table of the Lord in remembrance of Jesus, why should not all the members take turns in serving? The New Testament does not teach a limited priesthood, but it does teach that we are all priests unto God.

It would be refreshing to see the whole family involved. Couldn't even the very youngest Christians offer prayer? They do at our tables at home. And why not have children and young people as well as adults serving? Maybe in smaller congregations different families could lead from time to time in this ministry to others. Then we'd hear, "This morning the Brown family will serve Communion."

In recent years we've begun to realize that baptizing is not confined to an especially select group of ordained ministers. We ought to realize this about Communion as well. In fact, if we really started to practice this family approach to serving we would not get caught up in the idea that this is the primary responsibility of elders and deacons.

For people who profess a non-clerical, non-denominational position on Biblical matters, we could be more consistent by removing the ecclesiastical trappings that often surround the Lord's Supper.

"An Elder Must Be"

March 15, 1981

The qualifications for elders are set forth by Paul in the present tense. He says that "An overseer, then, must be above reproach, the husband of one wife, temperate, prudent, respectable, hospitable, able to teach, not addicted to wine or pugnacious, but gentle, uncontentious, free from the love of money. He must be one who manages his own household well, keeping his children under control with all dignity" (1 Timothy 3:2-4, *New American Standard Bible*).

I'm impressed with the fact that this is all set forth in the present tense: "must be." Paul did not say "must have been." He did not indicate that potential elders were responsible for these Christian qualities before they became Christians. Such a standard would mean that investigation into a prospective elder's pre-Christian life would be essential to determining his present qualifications for leadership. Who could pass such scrutiny?

In the light of this "must be," it is somewhat surprising that past marriage relationships often play a very dominant role in qualifying or disqualifying a man for the eldership. But do we ask whether a man before he became a Christian, was contentious or a money grabber or hospitable? In fact, I haven't heard of that money grabber problem being examined even in regard to a man's present Christian life. Often financial success is set forth as a commendation for leadership. Do we poke around very much into how people have become financially successful?

Indeed, a man's sullied past, in some people's thinking, may raise our estimation of him. If a person was intemperate enough in the past so that his conversion seems a prize of redemption, he is considered more qualified just because of this past intemperance.

Certainly, pre-Christian conduct in a community may have so tainted a man's reputation that he cannot be counted as above reproach in that community. But we should be careful that we do not automatically disqualify him on this assumption. Generally, non-Christians couldn't care less.

Paul's emphasis on "must be" ought to warn us against an emphasis on "must have been." Otherwise, we may open the door for remembering, even digging up, old sins and failures that God has already forgiven.

At Last, I've Seen It!

March 7, 1982

I waited a long time, years in fact, to see it happen. But it did happen. In a worship service of an orthodox, New Testament, restoration, Christian church I saw women come forward and serve Communion. It was a first in that congregation, as I suppose it would be in many of our congregations. But on that Sunday the tradition of only men serving the Lord's Supper was broken.

Why is it taking so long to sort New Testament doctrine from our traditions? There is nothing in the New Testament that spells out how the Lord's Supper is to be served or who is to serve. There is nothing about the many little plastic throw-away cups nor the professionally manufactured bite-sized bread. And there is nothing about whether men or boys or girls or women should do the serving. Why then have we ritualized this service into a symbol of male leadership? The answer is tradition.

Since the tradition is so common, some church members come to think of elders and deacons as the only servants at Communion time. Maybe some Christians even assume that this is the sole role that these elected officials have. Worse still, maybe sometimes elders and deacons feel that they have fulfilled their responsibilities if they are always present when it is their turn to serve.

I'm quite familiar with a common objection: "But if we let women serve at the table, they will want to dominate the church." Really? Is there some evidence that they would want to dominate any more than the men who now serve at the table? Are they inherently inclined to be use such a simple service as a base for power and authority? I can't believe that.

Isn't it time that we strip the ecclesiastical trappings away from Communion to share in it as a family without thought for position or symbols of leadership? If this service must serve some other purpose than in memory of Him, then we have missed the point, the very essence of it. Why not let all the members share in the serving just as they do in the partaking? In our homes, we don't confine mealtime prayers to just Dad, do we? Isn't Communion a communion of the whole body?

Well, anyway, I was blessed and pleased to be in a service where the old tradition gave way. I hope it will happen more often.

"Voluntary" School Prayer

April 25, 1982

What is the issue in the current debate about public school prayer? Basically, it is the promotion of the idea that the law would provide for voluntary prayers. So what is that supposed to mean?

Obviously, those who talk about "voluntary" prayers aren't using that word in its customary way. If they were, there would be no issue to discuss nor reason to promote a law. No court in our land has ever made any decision affecting voluntary prayer, because that is impossible. Who can control voluntary prayer? If a student wants to pray, he prays. He doesn't have to stand up in the classroom with the attention of all his classmates to do this. He's praying to God, not to men. And he needn't kneel by his desk or even vocalize his prayer. We have no laws that limit voluntary prayers. No one can successfully control such prayer nor police it out of existence. No Christian student is forced to give up praying when he walks onto the school grounds or goes into his classroom.

So what would "voluntary" prayer be? Probably a public prayer prepared by local school officials, government bureaucrats, or leaders of the dominant religious group in the community. Doesn't sound very voluntary does it? The voluntary nature of this kind of prayer, it has been suggested, would be that those who did not want to participate could leave the classroom during the time the prayer was being offered. So it wouldn't be a voluntary prayer at all, only a voluntary acceptance or rejection of the practice.

Any way you cut it, that appears discriminatory. Students who are not a part of the majority are placed in an awkward, even embarrassing, position before their peers. Some might concede to the practice, damaging their conscience. After all, what child wants to be in the minority?

Why should we want government to get entangled with this? Why do we clamor for less government regulation through taxation, while at the same time seeking government input into our children's prayers? Will such prayers somehow stem national infidelity? It seems to me that we are much safer with the home and the church setting the patterns for the devotional life of the young and their religious instruction. Does anyone really believe that school prayers will be more effective than those offered in the church and in the family?

Some of us who pray, decry the secular nature of our society, and grieve over the sinful conduct of mankind are attracted by the idea of enforcing a bit of religion in our schools. But who becomes a Christian by enforced devotions? Who becomes more spiritual by regulated religion?

We can all practice voluntary prayer now, in and out of school, anywhere we are. I hope we don't trap ourselves into governmental promotion of religion under the misnomer of "voluntary prayer."

Helping Single-Parent Families

January 16, 1983

There are many reasons for the rapidly increasing number of single-parent families. Analysis of this in itself doesn't really get us very far nor does it accomplish anything in meeting the needs of these families. The fact is that a lot of mothers and fathers are bringing up children without the help of a mate.

Even when both parents are present and working together at parenting, the problems can often be difficult. When one must handle the work of two, the task can become almost impossible.

What if the immense resources of the church were brought to bear upon this problem? We have buildings, often well equipped with nurseries, playgrounds, and other facilities for children. Mostly, we use these facilities for Sunday activities. We have financial resources and talented people as well.

Imagine what assistance could be offered to single parents if these resources were mobilized to provide day care for preschoolers and after-school care for children of school age. Instead of Mom or Dad having to find places for their children somewhere else in the community, they would be able to bring the children to the church for this care. Here the youngsters would receive Christian love, example, and teaching. Furthermore, the costs could be held down. This is often a great burden to working single parents. Sometimes, mothers particularly, are driven to welfare and away from working just because they cannot make ends meet.

Single parents face very heavy burdens. Creative work on this problem by congregations can become a vital ministry of service and an opportunity to extend Christian witness to many who may come to know Him by how we minister to widows, orphans, widowers, single parents, and the children who by no fault of their own must grow up with only Mom or Dad.

CHAPTER FOUR
DOCTRINE

George knew Christian doctrine without being doctrinaire. He possessed a solid grasp of the tenets of the faith without being a theological bully. George saw knowledge of Christian doctrine as fostering a firm faith in a world that perpetually challenges it. Doctrine serves to correct and reprove us when necessary and brings a joy when one is in a dynamic and powerful relationship with Christ. George was fully aware that doctrine was inescapable for Christians. Yet he was concerned that the Church had lost its sense of importance for knowing and practicing its doctrinal precepts.

George was no doctrinal minimalist. He wrote extensively on a wide variety of Christian doctrines, including baptism, forgiveness, judgment, evangelism, repentance, and prayer. In an effort to bring the whole counsel of God to bear on the Christian life, George upheld the importance of Christian doctrine. For him the body of true Christian doctrine is the foundation of faith. He knew doctrine was a means to distinguish the faith from the myriad of competing voices that inhabit our world. In an age of rampant pluralism, Christian doctrine embedded in the heart leads to a life of faithful obedience to Christ. George forms this message with great expertise in the following articles.

He is Risen!

April 2, 1972

Not long ago I heard an atheist talk on what he believed. With considerable clarity and conviction he set forth his view that man is just a chemical phenomenon in a material universe. This is the atheistic point of view, a completely naturalistic view of man and his world. Bertrand Russell summarized it in his definition, "Man is an accidental collocation of atoms."

When you ask an atheist why the world is here and why it works, he says that those are meaningless questions. There is no "why" because nothing lies back of the physical universe; there is no spiritual dimension.

Ask an atheist about the resurrection of Christ, and he will relegate this to the field of religious myth. His argument? There can be no resurrection because there are no miracles. There are no miracles because there is no divine force to make them happen.

Christians believe otherwise. We are supernaturalists. Whether one likes it or not, this is the view of the Bible and of Jesus and His apostles. The Bible says that "God created the world." Jesus and His apostles accept this view of man and the world. They taught that Jesus, God's Son, came to earth to redeem man. His life is proved divine by a whole series of miracles testifying to His power over all things. The resurrection of Christ is the crowning act of this career marked by miracle after miracle.

The atheist rejects this evidence and so he remains an atheist. The Christian accepts this evidence, and so he is a Christian. A simple, but profound, difference. So what's my point? We can't believe a thing as astounding as the resurrection of Christ without being changed by this. That change means a total commitment to Him who is our Savior and Lord, "declared to be the Son of God with power . . . by the resurrection from the dead" (Romans 1:4).

"I'm Praying for You"

February 18, 1973

Did you ever tell someone "I'll pray for you" and then remember weeks later that you'd forgotten to fulfill your promise? Or have you had someone tell you "I'm praying for you," and then you wondered if this was really so, or was it only pious words?

Experience teaches us that it is very easy to say things like this to one another. We learn the correct religious phrases for each situation and we may even sincerely say them, but performance is something else. It's really easier to say "I'm praying for you" than to pray for a brother or sister.

An old-fashioned, time-honored system can be of genuine help to any Christian who seriously wants to be a responsible prayer-warrior in bringing others' needs before the Lord. This is the prayer list. One just writes down on a paper, or a card, or a notebook the names of people to pray for, and then at the selected time, one by one, he brings these people and their needs before the Lord in prayer.

I label my card "Prayer List" and I keep it with the Bible I read at my times of prayer and devotion. The card reminds me of the people I'm concerned for; I can see them each one, as I pray for them. With the list I do not forget.

Now I'm sure that some will feel that this is a very mechanical system for doing something that I ought to do without the list. Maybe so. But the list does help. Communion is also a reminder. It is important because it is a reminder. This world in Satan's hands is constantly trying to get us to forget Jesus. He gave us the Supper to help us remember Him.

Of course, the prayer list doesn't rank with Communion as a spiritual exercise, but it has one purpose in common with Communion. It keeps us from forgetting. So when you say you are going to pray for someone, may I suggest that you write this in your prayer list?

I'm sure you'll discover with millions of others that the prayer list will aid you in sharing your life with others in prayer.

We Know

April 8, 1973

Did you ever read the book of 1 John through just looking for the things that John says about what Christians know? I counted fifteen verses in this little book where John says "we know" or "you know." What's so important about this? Just this: In John's time a philosophical sect called "Gnostics" claimed to have a special knowledge which common, simple Christians did not have. Their very name, "Gnostic," came from the Greek word meaning "knowledge." They thought they had a direct, spiritual pipeline to God and proudly held that others really didn't know Jesus or God's purposes.

They argued that everything material was evil and that only the spiritual was good. One part of this sect proclaimed that it didn't really matter how one lived as long as he believed the right things. The other part claimed that through ascetic discipline of the flesh one could cause the spirit to triumph.

So you see that when John wrote to the church he was assuring Christians that they had real knowledge of Christ, who had come in the flesh. They weren't the ignoramuses that the Gnostics claimed them to be. And John strongly connected that knowledge with obedience and Christian conduct: "We know that we have come to know him, if we keep his commandments. He who says he knows him and does not keep his commandments is a liar and the truth is not in him" (1 John 2:3, 4).

Furthermore, John emphasized that "you know that he was set forth to take away sins" (1 John 3:5). Jesus came to save men from their sins, not to allow them to live in sin. And He did not urge that by ascetic discipline man could cleanse himself of evil.

John asserted that Christians have real knowledge of Jesus through the testimony of the apostles, and that this knowledge leads to Christian living. The Gnostics were wrong in claiming to know Christ without a change in conduct.

Today many people tend to put down knowledge in favor of faith. John pulls knowledge and faith together. He shows us that Christians have a body of historical information about Jesus. Knowledge of this leads to faith, and faith leads to personal commitment and Christian conduct.

Opening Doors for Jesus

July 22, 1973

How can we confront others with the gospel? That was the question under discussion in an adult Sunday school class that I attended several months ago. All kinds of problems, rationalizations, and excuses were being discussed when a fine elder suggested that we were emphasizing the difficulties: "We don't witness because we get to thinking that others won't listen. We've decided that we are going to fail before we try." Then he shared a most interesting personal experience.

One of the men with whom this elder has regular business dealings is very profane. Every other word is a demonstration of his extra-dictionary vocabulary. So my elder friend had been wondering how to confront this man with Christ. "Just about the unlikeliest prospect I could think of," he said.

One day, Mr. Profane comes in with a business problem. Our elder hears this problem explained with all the regular linguistic embellishments. Then he manufactured his own little bombshell. "If it should turn out that I can't help you with this problem, could you pray about it and get an answer?"

"What did you say?" the surprised Mr. Profane stammered.

"I said that if it should turn out that I couldn't help you with your problem, could you pray about it and get an answer?"

"I don't pray very much."

"I know that. But could you pray about this problem and get an answer?"

"I used to pray, but I haven't in a long time."

"Well, think about it." That ended the first stage of this confrontation.

Sometime later Mr. Profane came in with a confession. "You really shook me up the last time I was in here. I've done a lot of thinking. You know, I'm trying to stop swearing."

The point is simple. Even the most unlikely person has a need for God. Obviously, Mr. Profane needs a lot more help, but that initial confrontation has opened a door. Courage, sensitivity, and a bit of imagination coupled with faith can reach hearts that may seem closed to us. Jesus in our lives can speak to others, if we let Him.

Nor Barbarian

September 23, 1973

The Greeks called people who could not speak Greek "barbarians." Originally, this word meant "one who stutters," and then it came to mean "one who makes unintelligible sounds." It was but a short step from that to its application to people who spoke languages other than Greek. They spoke "strange languages."

The next step was to think of people who spoke a "strange language" as "strange people." Not only did the Greeks see all others as different, but as inferior in culture and ones to be kept at a distance. They neatly stereotyped non-Greeks as "barbarians."

Alexander the Great pulled the ancient world together somewhat by making Greek the universal language, but he did not succeed in eliminating the prejudice against foreigners. Greek dominated other languages. The Greeks expected others to know their language; but they weren't interested in barbarian tongues.

Linguistic scientist Max Muller says that there was no linguistic science until "barbarian" was replaced by "brother." The gospel of Christ made this dramatic change. As soon as people became brothers in Jesus, they wanted to know each other, to share, to talk. The other man's language is no longer a "strange tongue" of an inferior people when that other man is your brother.

Dedicated men have now translated the Bible into hundreds of tongues and dialects and have given millions of people a written language and literacy. Christ has made us brothers. Therefore, there are no barbarians.

If we will make such an effort to cross the language barriers to reach our brothers, should we not also make the same effort to communicate with each other when we speak the same language? Shouldn't husbands and wives, children and parents, adults and youth, black and white, rich and poor—in short, all Christians—strive to destroy every false division that separates us? We are brothers, not barbarians.

In Remembrance

January 18, 1976

How do you remember Jesus during communion time? The recent holiday season reminded me that much of what is involved in that season comes from memory. We invest Christmastime with family memories and traditions—exchanging gifts, preparing special foods, visits, and a whole host of festive decorations that bind our family units together and keep us related to our corporate past.

In Christian families we specifically find our thought of Jesus' birth a joyous remembrance of God's sacrificing love, and we are bound to God who acted for us through Jesus. We celebrate our Christian history in worship. We sing the Christmas carols and are spiritually warmed.

But we do not remember just one thing. We don't just remember a special family pastry, or we don't just think alone of the birth of Christ. These are events that are parts of larger patterns of remembrance. The pastry recipe has been handed down for several generations; it is connected with all our Christmas memories. So Christ's birth is connected with His life, His sacrifice, and His ministry for us now.

So when we come to the Lord's table to remember Him we do not just remember when He instituted the supper, or that He told us to do this in His remembrance. Even His death is not remembered alone. The whole scope of His life and purpose comes into view.

We know that the elements speak of our salvation by His sacrifice. They tell us that we are one body in Him—a family. They urge upon us a measurement of our own lives in the light of His. They call us to sacrifice self for Him and for the needs of others.

You see, we remember Jesus as the one who is central to every area of our living. Doing this adds fullness and blessing to our lives. It's not just the cross, or the birth, or the resurrection, or our salvation, or His coming again, or His teaching that makes communion memory precious. It's all of these things and much more—all that we are able to know and appreciate as we grow—that makes "in remembrance of me" a precious time at the beginning of each new week.

Safety Not Guaranteed

May 22, 1977

The position of the herald, or message carrier, was sacred in ancient Greece. When the Megarians violated this code and murdered a herald sent from Athens, the Athenians resolved never again to send a herald to them. Furthermore, Athenian generals conducted two predatory raids on the Megarians every year.

The heralds carried official messages for people in authority. To do damage to them was to disrupt and destroy communications. To serve in this capacity the herald needed a strong, clear voice and was not supposed to exaggerate. He was to give the messages accurately, adding and taking away nothing.

It is interesting that heralds who played such an important part in Greek life do not play such a part in the New Testament world. Why not? Wouldn't it seem that the apostles and Christian evangelists should merit this title?

The Bible uses the word not to name the people who preach, but to name the message. Christ came into the world as the Word of God; His followers declare Him to others. None of the people who serve Him are promised an immunity from dangers or worldly scorn. In fact, He warned that the world that rejected Him would reject His proclaimers.

His messengers are like sheep among wolves. They must proclaim His Word and accept the consequences for this. God does not promise to protect them. Persecutions have been mounted again and again against His followers. So, since there are no persons in His kingdom sacred and inviolable to the world, the office of herald is almost unknown in the New Testament.

But even with the protection that the herald received, Jesus' messengers have given and are giving His message to the world. The ancient heralds spoke for earthly kings. Jesus, the Heavenly King, sends forth His proclaimers into our world. Mandatory still is the obligation to give the message clearly and strongly, adding nothing, subtracting nothing. And it is important that while we skillfully use all means available to declare His Word, we do not become so enamored with human devices and rhetorical powers that we bring the attention to ourselves. He is the Savior. We are His messengers. "We preach not ourselves but Christ the Lord" (2 Corinthians 4:5).

Questions or Answers?

October 30, 1977

Frankly, I was amazed to read a whole book (all 187 pages) on the subject *How to Be Born Again* and not read the word baptism one time. Furthermore, when the actual steps for conversion are listed, only six Scriptures are given, and none of those are from the Acts of the Apostles. And even when the conversion of the three thousand on Pentecost is described, not one verse from Acts is used. Instead, John 5:24 is used to conclude the description: "Truly, truly, I say to you, he who hears My word, and believes Him who sent Me, has eternal life, and does not come into judgment, but has passed out of death into life."*

This is not to say that Billy Graham's book *How to be Born Again* has no useful information. But it is obviously incomplete in terms of its title. How can one write on this subject without including the conversion accounts given in Acts? Here people were born again, and we see how this took place. And we can't leave out Jesus' own instructions about being born again and pretend to have a complete treatment of the subject.

This raises the question of how we determine the Bible teaching on any matter. Do we start from a deductive position, having the answer already in mind and seek support in the Bible? Or should we start from an inductive position, having a question and the seek the answer in Scripture? I am convinced the only sound way is to seek answers. Otherwise, having already determined the answer, we will ignore contrary evidence because we do not want our answer disturbed.

How to be born again cannot be explained by leaving out Jesus' instructions to his disciples or their fulfillment of those instructions as given in Acts. Biblical study must start with the questions, not with the answers.

New American Standard Bible, © 1972 by the Lockman Foundation, used by permission.

"Not Baptizing Them"

November 4, 1979

A recent issue of *Eternity* (June 1979) quotes William McColley, formerly with Inter-Varsity: "When I left Inter-Varsity one of the reasons was the Great Commission. As IVCF was promulgating it, it was 'Go ye into all the world and make disciples of all nations not baptizing them because we can't agree on that, but teaching them only the things we can agree on.'"

Obviously, if we tried to fulfill the Commission only by baptizing people, that would fall far short of what Jesus commanded. To teach all that He commanded is very demanding. In fact, we are probably all failures at this. The maturity in the Word that this requires takes a long time to achieve, if it can be achieved at all. It's so easy to miss something, distort something, or just plain fail to understand all the implications of something that He taught.

But admission of failure at this level cannot possibly excuse us for deliberately refusing to fulfill a command specifically stated. He did say "baptizing them." Nothing can change that. It is plain in Scripture that the apostles followed this command.

Several years ago I was discussing this point with a young preacher who claimed that to insist on baptism was to add to the gospel! I asked him about all the examples in Acts and he countered with "Well, what is Acts, just a history." And that is precisely the point. It is from that history of apostolic action that we can find the norms for our practice. Do doctors avoid medical books that cite case histories in favor of those that give only interpretations? Don't lawyers and judges go back to cases? They have bookshelves filled with volumes of case histories as examples. So Acts provides the cases when we want to find out about how people were saved in the first century, in the time of the apostles.

As much as we may admire the religious profession and practice of those who neglect the command to baptize, or as much as we may enjoy their music or their conferences and their fellowship, we still cannot ignore the fact that He said "baptizing them." He did not say "not baptizing them."

America's Fourth Religion

February 27, 1983

Generally, we identify the religious affiliations of Americans as Catholic, Protestant, or Jewish. But there has emerged a strong, extra option, one that many Americans now accept. Often people who are nominally participants in one of the three other religions actually embrace much of the thinking and philosophy of this fourth religion. Because of this, its dangers are subtle and powerful.

In a rather simple way we can describe the characteristics of this fourth American religion by noting its approach to six basic topics: God, man, the Bible, Christ, faith, and the church.

According to the view of those who are a part of this fourth religion, God is a power outside ourselves; out there somewhere is something, so we are not entirely abandoned.

Man is good, and sin is just an old myth about human behavior.

The Bible is not an inspired book, but it is a wonderful resource of ideas, ethics, intellectual insights, and literary beauty.

Christ was a remarkable charismatic personality. He was not divine, but He was a very superior human and marvelous model for our lives.

Faith is our search for meaning. The search itself may be the most important quality of faith.

The church is a good organization for people doing good things. In fact, the measure of value for any church is its involvement in doing good.

These viewpoints are quite appealing to many people. There is no demand for repentance or serious commitment. One has a religion that many think is quite nice and not too different from traditional religion. Many see nothing particularly threatening in this fourth religion, nor does it seem to be openly critical of what others may believe. "After all," its adherents would claim, "We do believe in God and the Bible."

The danger in these views is greater for us than in views that appear openly hostile and critical of the Christian faith. Religious language is used to describe a basically humanistic approach to life and meaning. If the devil can dilute Biblical faith, he wins just as well as he does by developing militant atheists.

Biblical Religion

March 6, 1983

Last week we took a look at the characteristics of what I call America's fourth religion. We looked at six topics (God, man, the Bible, Christ, faith, and the church) to see how people employ religious language to describe what amounts to unbiblical humanism. Let's try today to give brief Biblical views on each of these topics.

1) God. The Bible teaches from opening page that God is the creator, that He cares for man, provides for all his needs, and in His son, Jesus, provides for man's eternal salvation. God is not just a force or power. He is personal.

2) Man. Man fell from God's plan for him, became a sinner, and is now the object of God's love in the salvation provided in Jesus. That salvation is attained only as we repent and obey the gospel.

3) The Bible. This is God's revealed Word for us. He has spoken authoritatively and confirmed the binding nature of His covenants with us again and again.

4) Christ. He is the promised Messiah of the Old Testament. He was born miraculously of Mary and the Holy Spirit. He gave His life as a ransom for sin, was raised from the dead in victory over the grave, and ascended to the right hand of the Father. He ministers for us as our high priest.

5) Faith. Faith is believing that God is and that He is the rewarder of all those who seek after Him. Faith is not a human quest for God, but a response to God who has revealed himself to us in nature, in the Bible, and in His Son.

6) The church. The church is the body of Christ, made up of all the redeemed. Jesus is the head of the church and had complete authority over His body. The church is more than a society for doing good; it has been entrusted with the mission of taking the gospel to all the world.

I'm not trying to write a creed. I'm just trying to make a contrast. Biblical Christianity is very different from every other religion, including America's fourth religion. We have the responsibility to evangelize the world and to defend the faith. We cannot do that unless we understand what others believe and clarify in our own minds exactly what it is that we believe.

Every Christian ought to be able to give a clear and simple explanation of Biblical teaching on the basics. America's fourth religion will not just go away; it must be confronted with the truth.

How About Theistic Gravity?

June 12, 1983

If the case were fully closed scientifically and theologically on the process or processes by which all life forms have come into existence, then there could be no difference between the scientific and religious views. God gave us both books, the book of nature and the revelation we know as the Bible. They would not be found inconsistent in themselves or with each other if the case could be completely closed by adequate information on the development of the forms of life, the creation process.

But that's the rub. The Bible doesn't give scientific evidence on the creation process, and, on the other hand, nature yields up her secrets piecemeal and very slowly. Much of the evidence we would like to have may never become available. Even the case for and against some kind of evolutionary process is incomplete. There seems to be inadequate scientific evidence to fully settle this matter and inadequate Biblical evidence to rule with certainty either for or against the evolutionary hypothesis.

Biblically, of course, we reject the idea of the existence of the natural order separate from God the Creator. We cannot accept a naturalistic interpretation. This is why Christians who favor the evolutionary hypothesis often call themselves "theistic evolutionists." They mean by this that evolution may have been the process that God used to develop all life from the dust of the earth.

It's rather interesting that we never feel obligated to talk of theistic gravity or theistic entropy or theistic theories of light and electricity. Why not? People who reject God and explain everything naturalistically exclude God from gravity and entropy too, just as they do from evolutionary theories. Still we do not feel it necessary for us to capture these theories for God by categorizing them as theistic.

Our difficulty is not so much with theories that we use in seeking to find the secret of how things work, but in the overall view of whether the natural system is closed or open. Did it make itself? Does it have the power to perpetuate itself? Or is the natural system made by God, kept running by Him and destined for a final purpose by Him?

Once we embrace the Biblical view, "In the beginning God created," then everything is theistic and using that label is redundant.

Don't Stop at 490

May 27, 1984

"You mean I'm supposed to forgive him 490 times?" That does seem a bit excessive, doesn't it? But that's what Jesus said. We know that He wasn't really talking numbers at all. That "seventy times seven" was Jesus' response to Peter's question, "Lord, how often shall my brother sin against me and I forgive him?" (Matthew 18:21, *New American Standard Bible*). Then the Lord went on to tell a story about forgiveness and concluded that there will be no mercy from God for those who do not forgive from the heart. If we are to be like our Father, we must be forgiving.

Face it, we all need forgiveness. There is no way to get through this life without offending, wronging, even at times hurting others. We see things differently from others, so we argue and contend and sometimes alienate others by our attitudes. Often we seek what others are also seeking, so we compete and struggle for a promotion, for a bit more of the pie, to be first at the intersection, or to win the game.

Neglecting to show our gratitude for undeserved favors, we grieve those who have gone out of their way or expense to help us. Promising to fulfill responsibilities, we shirk them, letting others down and burdening them with our failures. Responding to stress with immature emotionalism, we shock and offend those whom we love the most.

Over and over again, 490 times and *more*, we need both the forgiveness of God and the forgiveness of our families, friends, and neighbors.

How little of us to ask whether we are responsible for forgiving *seven* times when we ourselves are in need of much, much more forgiveness than that for our own offenses. Jesus tells us that God's children forgive others from their hearts. It is not a matter of law or duty, but a response that comes naturally to those who have received His great pardon and who recognize that "all have sinned" (Romans 3:21). In forgiving, we act like our Father and show that we are His children.

'Faith Plus Nothing'

March 24, 1985

He made it quite clear in his sermon that he'd been baptized, but he hastened on to say that, of course, this had nothing to do with his salvation. I found this somewhat peculiar and decided to discuss this with him after the meeting was over.

When I asked him about passages in Acts dealing with baptism, he quickly responded, "But what is Acts? It's just a history of the church."

"Yes, I know," I said. "Are you suggesting that this book isn't important because it's just a history of the early church?" He wasn't ready to get into that corner and submitted that it was a valuable book all right, but that he hadn't studied it very much.

Steadily he resisted acceptance of the texts I read that dealt with baptism. Over and over again, he repeated this assertion: "We are saved by faith plus nothing!"

I wanted him to show me where that idea was expressed in Scripture, for I continue to believe that if an idea is Scriptural then it must appear somewhere in the language of the Bible. Failing to get any satisfactory answers about this, I asked my very confident young preacher if "plus nothing" would mean that we are saved by faith apart from repentance, the blood of Christ, and personal confession.

This line of questioning only led to frustration. Since, obviously, we couldn't leave out such important items from salvation, the bold "plus nothing" was, in modern governmental language, becoming "inoperative."

So I wondered now if he would accept what Peter said on Pentecost: "Repent, and let each of you be baptized in the name of Jesus Christ for the forgiveness of your sins; and you shall receive the gift of the Holy Spirit" (Acts 2:38). Immediately he was ready to correct this obviously wrong translation. I heard him out. "The preposition here translated *for* should be translated *on the basis of*. Greek prepositions often have several different meanings, and in this context the correct meaning is *on the basis of*." He told me that good scholars of the Greek had enlightened him on this in the seminary where he had studied.

I decided to make one more attempt. "Well," I said, "what should we do then in translating Matthew 26:28? The English text reads, "For this is My blood of the covenant, which is poured out for many for forgiveness of sins." I went on to explain, "By your principle that the preposition *for* should be translated *on the basis of*, we would have Jesus dying on the cross not for the forgiveness of sins, but because they had already been forgiven! How does that work out?

"This is a very different situation," he assured me. "The translation is correct here."

"But in the Greek the same words are used in both texts in exactly the same order. Why is one right and the other wrong?"

"Because we are saved by faith plus nothing. Baptism just can't have anything to do with remission of sins. If it did, then we'd be saved by faith plus baptism; that's impossible."

I knew that we'd come full circle now and that we weren't going to get this matter settled in this brief discussion.

"I know that we're not going to get this settled tonight," I said. "Thanks for talking with me."

"Sir," he replied, "before we part, I must tell you that you are a heretic, for you are adding to the Word of God. This is serious and very dangerous. I pray that you'll change your ways and accept the truth."

On that dismal note, our conversation ended.

Scripture quotes in this column are from the *New American Standard Bible.*

Not An Option

April 7, 1985

The proclamation of the resurrection is not an option for us who are Christians. It's on this point that many years ago I received my first jolt from the liberal religious press. I was a young preacher, just beginning my ministry, when I read some stuff that simply amazed me. It was in a publication for high schoolers that I read something like this: "The disciples were greatly discouraged after Jesus was crucified. They felt that all their hopes had died and been buried with their leader. They were deeply burdened with this gloom. Then on Sunday morning, they realized that such a life as Jesus had lived could never be destroyed. They knew that He would live on in their hearts. He had been raised again in them."

At that time I knew very little about the subtleties of theology, but I was able to read through those lines. This was no affirmation of His resurrection. This was just a claim for human psychological resilience and rationalization. Instinctively I knew that this would never be enough for me. Either He was raised and vindicated as the Son of God with power, or He is still in the grave and we are, in Paul's words, "of all most most miserable."

Anyone reading the New Testament for the first time will find an abundance of affirmations on the resurrection. The apostles didn't quibble on this. They hung their case for Jesus being the Messiah and the Savior on this mighty act.

Today we throng to churches to express our faith in His power over our greatest enemies: death, sin, and the grave. The music, the decorations, the preaching, and the prayers all serve to lift up that great truth, that cornerstone of Christian conviction.

The resurrection is not optional to Biblical teaching and preaching. Without the resurrection there is no Savior, no good news, no salvation, and no hope of Heaven.

We are not engaged in psychological games today. He is risen!

Discerning the Body

October 20, 1985

When the prodigal son returned home, his father gave a feast that his older brother refused to attend. The very act of sitting at the table and sharing food was a profession of forgiveness and acceptance. The older son was not ready for that.

In many countries and cultures, breaking bread together is an act of brotherliness, a way of acceptance. When a king or a great ruler invites a deposed political rival or a dismissed servant back to the table, he shows forgiveness.

When we come to the Lord's table, we must all accept one another if that meal is to be entered into meaningfully. When we discern His body, we know that it is *His* body, that *He* paid for it with *His* blood, and that we are obligated to remember Him and accept the bonds that hold us together because of *His* sacrifice.

If we give only the slightest amount of time to this remembrance (sometimes less than we do the announcements or the special music), can we wonder why we suffer in our own small shells of self-centeredness, pride, and antagonism? When the Corinthians failed to discern the body, they became weak and sickly.

Spiritually, the most potent force for unity that we share is the Lord's meal. Are we so afraid of this power that we reduce our way of participation to an exercise in efficiency and brevity while we fail in openness to each other?

What if we began to discern each other's needs, each other's anxieties, fears, and physical concerns? Would we find that there would be a sharing of food, of clothing, of money, of shelter, of transportation, of time?

Our society is radically devoted to individuality and independence. The Lord's Supper clashes with this idea. It cries out for mutuality, brotherhood, understanding, fellowship, empathy, sharing, forgiveness, encouragement, tears, and love.

Rituals are safe and manageable. A real family meal is not a ritual. It may take some effort to change our traditions so that we can discern the body. But such effort will be richly rewarded in the restoration of the power of the meaning of this meal and in the unity of the body in the Spirit and in love.

Shall we try?

CHAPTER FIVE
PRACTICAL LIVING

An elder, professor, father, husband, grandfather, citizen, preacher, and scholar—George Alder possessed that rare quality that enabled him to bridge the theoretical and practical with rare ease. There was little patience with intellectual snobbery or unreflected passion. His was a focused, thoughtful, and always useable common sense about life, family, current events, and human nature. Keenly aware and like us engaged in ongoing everyday tasks, he regularly pointed out irony, contradiction, inconsistency, and the humorous in everyday life situations to colleagues, students, family and any who would listen. George never forgot a joke or a funny story—and was "famous" for the ability to illustrate any life situation with one. Comfortable in the Academy, at church, on the backpack trail, at home, or in travel, he rarely missed the opportunity to connect those environments and experiences to his faith and the realities of everyday living. We are indebted to his insights and common sense.

Demonstrating Your Faith

November 24, 1968

A shouting minority refusing to allow a speaker to be heard by those who want to hear him is a disgraceful demonstration in a democratic society. The whole thing is completely contrary to the ideal of free speech. But, even though we strive in our country to guarantee the right to speak, we cannot guarantee a considerate hearing. The right to speak is a constitutional right; the right to be heard must be earned. And it is also true that the right to speak for and about Jesus Christ belongs to all Christians, but we must earn a hearing. How?

First, let's keep in mind that people listen to people, not to words. We believe people, not their words. The person who speaks gives meaning to his words by what he is. If we try to perfect some neat little speech for telling people about Christ, we may fail to reach them. If we develop our understanding of Christ in our own lives, then we will have something vital to share. We must be genuine Christian persons in order to make Christ real to someone else. It's not techniques we need, but a deep relationship with the Lord.

Second, in order to get anyone to listen attentively we must show genuine respect and love for that person. Only when our words are matched by a sincere effort to help someone else will those words be effective. We are all very sensitive to this. This means that the motivation to win others to the Lord must always be that motivation based upon the faith that every person is one "for whom Christ died."

To be heard we have to go beyond knowing a story. The story could be put on a phonograph record. God wants witnesses who share the faith out of a life of faith. Others want to know not only who Jesus is, but what He means to one who has accepted Him. We don't go forth as lawyers to argue people into accepting Christ, but we are witnesses demonstrating what it means to know Him.

"Whosoever"

January 19, 1969

A magazine cartoon pictured two hippies in a park. One asked, "Do you love me?"

"Of course," the other replied, "I love everybody."

The golden text of the Bible, John 3:16, is more personal than that: "For God so loved the world that he gave his only begotten son that whosoever believeth on him should not perish but have eternal life." Possibly that one pronoun, "whosoever," has provided more encouragement than any other single word in the Bible. Everybody wants to be loved and accepted and valued. This great text opens the door to all.

Much that makes up our Western society conspires against persons. We have massive factories, supersized universities, and complex impersonal governmental machinery. Justice Douglas of the United States Supreme Court says that our hardest task in the rest of this century will be to protect the individual from big government.

This very bigness in institutions tends to minimize the importance of persons. In Jesus' day Rome was big and powerful; persons were expendable. Large-scale building projects, massive organization, and tremendous military exploits characterized that time. Thousands of people were used up as slaves for the state.

What a contrast to this disregard for life was Jesus' emphasis upon persons! Busy as He was He always took time for people. That's why He came. It is this emphasis that Christians must make today. The gospel is personal, not institutional. To people frustrated with the unresponsive nature of large institutions the message of Christ is "I died for you." The church, Christ's body on earth, is made up of individuals. And it is as individuals that we must show His love to others. We must go beyond that hippie "I love everybody" attitude, to Christ's personalized "whosoever" expression of love.

How About Your Morals

October 19, 1969

How about your morals in our modern Babylonian society? Max Lerner says that our society is "perhaps more Babylonian than Babylon itself." So permissive, in fact, have we now become that films, plays, pop songs, magazines and paperbacks, and commercials spew forth a constant, blatant, taboo-shattering emphasis on sex. Some call this breakdown of restraint "freedom," others hail it as "progress," and still others lament it as "decadence."

The snag is not in the names we give it, nor even in the meaning of the moral revolution. The real problem is in what happens to people who abdicate their responsibility for making moral judgments. Permissive attitudes in sex are not making happier people. This permissiveness seems to be the open door to the old Pandora's box of sensualism.

This sensate emphasis is not a new thing. Paul faced it in the Graeco-Roman culture of his day. His denunciation of such sensualism in Romans, chapter one, could have been directed to our time. In his letters, Paul contrasts the morals of unredeemed man with the morals of the redeemed. Now, as then, whether or not the masses yield to God's requirements for purity, respect for others as well as self, and obedience to His commands, Christians come under the exhortation "present your bodies a living sacrifice, holy, acceptable to God, which is your logical service."

Why is this our "logical" service? Precisely because every effort of man, at self-redemption, reform, adjustment, or whatever he calls it, comes to failure. Only in Jesus do we find the way of cleansing, power and wholeness. And this reliance on Him is not an attempt to bury temptations, but to squarely face and recognize them.

Every temptation is directed to the misuse of some human potential. The massive emphasis today is to the misuse of sex. The Bible does not urge a rejection of sex. The Bible urges a proper, sanctified, responsible use of this life force. When consecrated to God the sexual function brings joy and happiness. When misused by Satan it brings misery and sadness.

How about your morals? They're going to have to be better quality than the mass product today if you wish to live your life as a Christian.

Is That All There Is?

January 25, 1970

A popular song raises the question, "Is That All There Is?" The lamentation is that the varied experiences of life—going to a circus, seeing a fire, and being disappointed in love—offer no real meaning for life. In fact, these experiences lead to a feeling of emptiness and almost cynical despair. Of course, the very fact that the question is raised suggests that we feel there really should be more, that perhaps we are missing something.

The song suggests the escape, "Let's break out the booze and have a ball." Now it's pretty obvious that booze, drugs, sex, and entertainment do not satisfy. When soberness returns, when the trip is ended, when passion cools, when the show is over, that haunting question will still be there: "Is that all there is?"

Some three thousand years ago Solomon tried about everything available to overcome boredom, despair, and painful longing. In the book of Ecclesiastes in the Old Testament he tells about his efforts to find the answer. At the beginning of his book he says: "All things are full of weariness ... The eye is not satisfied with seeing, nor the ear with hearing" (Ecclesiastes 1:8). Everything seemed dull to him.

He tried to find happiness through laughter, he enjoyed luxurious houses, gathered treasures, indulged his senses, and had the best in food and drink. His conclusion was that he still felt empty, that nothing really helped. He called all these things "vanity," meaning empty.

But he did find an answer at last. After years of futile searching and experimenting he concluded: "This is the end of the matter; all hath been heard: Fear God, and keep his commandments; for this is the whole duty of man" (Ecclesiastes 12:13). He had discovered that life has meaning when it is lived in obedience to and in love for God. Life without faith is empty, with faith it is full. No, that's not all there is, there is much, much more.

"Do Your Own Thing"

July 2, 1972

The modern statement of freedom and tolerance is "do your own thing." This seems to mean that no one need get caught in trying to live like others, do what others would like, or subscribe to any laws. It promises that freedom will be known by doing what one desires or values by his own standards, not by the standards of others. "Do your own thing" wouldn't be a bad motto if it only meant to live your own life, be a real person. But if it implies, as I believe it does, a kind of wholesale promise of happiness in freedom, then we may well question if the promise implied can be fulfilled.

Can you really do your own thing? Can you live in such freedom that you are really free? Are there hidden traps set to catch us when we try to do our own thing? How many smokers started out to do their own thing and would like now to be free? How many drug addicts and alcoholics got hooked by trying to be free?

The problem is that whenever we try to live with self in the center of all our judgments and actions we soon end up not liking the self whom we express, and others don't like us either. Adam and Eve first heard that counsel, "Do your own thing; you can be as smart as God; you don't need His rules to live by." They tried it. And they soon hated it.

We suspect that often when "do your own thing" is advised someone is actually trying to get us to do *his* thing. The drug pushers have never shown any real interest in anyone else's personal freedom. The liquor trade isn't flourishing by promoting maturity.

The sad story of the book of Judges is about a nation of people attempting to live without civil law or divine law. They got into bondage again and again. God had to keep helping them. The last verse in that book is a pithy summary, "In those days there was no king in Israel: every man did that which was right in his own eyes" (Judges 21:25).

As Unto the Lord

December 10, 1972

It is fashionable now to criticize the so-called "Protestant work ethic." It is claimed that the work ethic has fixed upon man a demanding burden to labor and achieve. Captured now by this demand, he cannot free himself to enjoy leisure, and in the face of the fact that the sixty-hour work week has shrunk to forty and will soon shrink to twenty-five, how will man be able to adjust and accept this new freedom?

A couple of points are missed in this plausible sounding attack. First, the main idea in the work ethic came from Luther's understanding that there is no sacred-secular division in life. God is concerned as much with what a man does in the field or the shop or the office as He is with what he does in church on Sunday. Therefore, every Christian labors and worships "as unto the Lord." The apostle Paul even advocates that Christians who happened to be slaves should honor the Lord in their lives.

The second thing to think about is this: It is true that people may not be happier with more leisure time, nor know how to use this time, but that's not because of the "Protestant work ethic," it's because they are working with God left out of their lives.

What kind of world would it be if everyone, workman, artist, professional man, etc., did everything to glorify God? Every task, regardless of how menial, would bestow honor and dignity upon the laborer.

This is what Christians are urged to do. We are not to compartmentalize life, so that on Sunday we honor God, but complain all week about the work we do. That's all wrong. The "Protestant work ethic" truly understood is not a burden on man, but a motivation for all work in the understanding that all of life is lived for God.

It isn't the work ethic then that is destroying man. It's enslavement to the values of this world separated from God that's the real problem. The work ethic separated from God is an endorsement of materialism. When men work as unto the Lord all of life is changed. And in a world lost in sin, there will be plenty for every Christian to do even with a twenty-five hour work week.

"Bless This Food": Ritual or Reverence?

August 26, 1973

We had just raised our heads from our mealtime prayer when he asked his question, "Why do we do this?" That began a discussion that lasted through our lunch period. Quite soon we all agreed that mealtime prayers can easily become little, ritualistic, oft-repeated monologues, empty of meaning, even lacking in reverence. But we also agreed that this should not be so.

Our discussion produced a number of good reasons for mealtime prayers. Let me share several of them with you. In these prayers we acknowledge our dependence upon God not only for food, but for everything. Food is a very direct link to God, for every day, two, three, or four times, we get hungry and eat. We know that without food we would perish. In prayer before we take food we thank God for His providence in animals, plants, earth, water, air, and sunlight sustained.

Mealtime prayers also help us to remember that while we share in the bounties of the earth it is inconsistent to thank God for food and in the moments following indulge our appetites to the point of gluttony. What hypocrisy it would be to thank God for food to sustain our lives and then use that good to destroy the body!

Furthermore, gratitude expressed at mealtime prayers keeps us from wastefulness. The old idea of "cleaning your plate," of taking no more than necessary, comes to mind when we thank God for what He has given. Since He has supplied everything, we must be faithful stewards.

We also agreed that being sincerely prayerful could make us more conscious of the very nature of the food we eat, is it wholesome? Have we processed simple grains until they are no longer nutritious? Are we eating junk food with no real value to the body? Is our diet balanced to the needs of the body?

So to eat without praying is to miss in each day opportunities to draw close to God and to be thankful. That's a great loss. Mealtime prayers can descend to deadening ritual, but they can also ascend to highest reverence. We decide which they will be.

Judge Not

September 30, 1973

How quickly we quote Jesus' "Judge not," when we are seeking immunity from another's judgment. Yet, there probably isn't any command He gave that we more persistently violate and ignore. The briefest conversation will often and easily get involved in censorship. How many times such conversations begin, "Did you hear what Bill did?" or "Isn't she being stupid for getting engaged to a guy like that?" At the outset the conversation is a judgment and probably gossip as well.

We cut others down to size by measuring them from our personal base of superior morality, ethics, religion, politics, or good sense. Only constant watchfulness upon our own hearts and tongues can keep us obedient to Jesus' command.

We ought to obey His command for some very good reasons. We shouldn't judge, because we just aren't good judges. Usually we can't be fair, because we don't know all the facts. How easy it is to be critical of another when we don't know his burdens, his limitations, and his temptations.

Bitter criticism pushes out love and sympathy and destroys any possibility for real understanding. Concerned only with sharpening the barbs of criticisms and the arrows of slander, we do not stop for love and empathy.

Judgment isolates us from others and magnifies the spirit of judgment and faultfinding. Fellowship is destroyed, and hearts are broken by the lies that are passed off as truth. Sometimes, in a very cruel way we hide our criticism behind a smoke screen of humor so that our victims dare not respond lest they be accused of taking us seriously!

Jesus said that judgment brings judgment back upon the judge. Judgment begets judgment. Love and concern nurture love and concern. Only God can be judge. Of course, it is obvious to anyone that we all must discern whether others are qualified for jobs, honest in representing products, and the like. But Jesus has forbidden destructive judgment that assassinates the character of another in order to build up our own weak self-esteem. When He said "Judge not," He was talking to us.

Just Hanging Around

February 3, 1974

Did you ever feed a stray dog? That's all it takes to get him to hang around. Before long he's yours. You've acquired a pet without half trying. A stray dog will accept you quicker than you can adopt him. He needs very little encouragement to be a part of your family.

The writer of *Hebrews* describes sin in this way. In chapter twelve, verse one, he urges Christians to "lay aside every weight and the sin which so easily besets us." The phrase "which so easily besets" translates one Greek word made up of three separate words. These separate words can be translated "easily," "around" and "standing." Put together, the meaning is "which stands around easily." In a more vernacular form we could translate "hangs around."

Some commentators suggest that this sin that just hangs around is sin that we get familiar with because it is always present. Eventually, we make peace with it and fail to notice any evil in it at all. In the exaggerated moral simplicity of a television western the good guys are always clearly distinguished from the bad guys. In real life this is seldom so. Evil doesn't go around saying "Look, I'm bad. I'm wearing a black hat!" So this warning reminds us that evil may become a part of our lives just because it always hangs around.

Of course, if we never fed the stray dog, he'd wander on. Perhaps if we never made peace with ever present evil, it would lose its grip on life as well. Earlier in the Hebrew letter the writer shows that a sign of maturity is the ability to discern good from evil. This ability comes through exercise.

So, if we are to get rid of the sin that hangs around so we can run the race set before us, we will have to discern evil. How much of the world's emphasis on possessions do we accept, how much of its playboy sexual philosophy, how much of its foul language, its disregard for God, etc.? These are sins that hang around. We've got to be firm about these things or before long we will have as household pets those which at one time we only fed at the door.

Pressing On

October 13, 1974

One of my students asked me how to study. He wanted some "wisdom" on how to become successful in learning Greek. He's a sincere student and openly honest about himself and the problem he's having in study. He wasn't looking for magical tricks to an "A." His concern was how to apply himself to Greek so that he could really learn.

I shared with him some practical tips on study and then suggested a larger concept put forth by Philo about two thousand years ago. Philo divided his students into three groups, the *archomenoi*, *prokopontes*, and *teleoioi*. Translated, these terms mean beginners, the ones pressing on, and the mature.

We all have to begin somewhere to be Christians. We must be born anew, become babes in Christ, and then it's a matter for pressing on. There is just a lot of growing to be done before we become mature. God wants that maturity, but that's not the next step after one's becoming a Christian.

I started my study of Greek in 1942. So I've had thirty-two years at it, and I'm far from finished yet. I started studying German recently and that reminded me that the route from beginner to mature is long and difficult. That pressing on period is where we must persevere.

Many persons are deflected from maturity because maturity seems elusive and the pressing on is difficult and demanding. But it is in this in-between time where most of life is spent and where most of our accomplishments are achieved. Great musicians know that there is always a better performance. The athlete knows that every record can be broken. The Christian knows that maturity in Christ will be fully acquired only when Jesus comes to transform us into His likeness. So we aren't going to make an "A" by tricks: it is our task to live faithfully each day in a maturing experience as we wait for that great day when Jesus comes.

How Long to Make a Disciple?

March 9, 1975

"So we had a fantastic time witnessing to this guy that we met last night at McDonald's. He had never heard of Jesus. He'd tried drugs and everything, and then he opened up to us and by midnight he'd accepted the Lord. Praise God!"

Have you heard testimonies like that? They seem so moving. And it is great that people are witnessing of what Jesus means to them. But can a person who never heard of Jesus accept Him quite that quickly and easily? Would we marry someone after a two-hour conversation, or make a total career decision on the basis of the testimony of one successful person in that career?

The witness of several people that Jesus is real and the sharing of John 3:16 falls far short of a presentation of who Jesus is. How can we accept Him and become committed to Him without knowing who He is?

True, a swift confrontation with a defeated person, desperately trying to find some meaning in life, may be like a piece of wreckage floating toward a drowning, shipwrecked sailor. Who wouldn't reach out and take it?

So he says "I accept Jesus in my heart." Then there are tears, hugs, and hallelujahs. But to bring that person to Jesus is a whole lot tougher than that. The quick confrontation may give personality a radical shock. Gospel bombs detonated within the life may upset one to say "I accept Jesus." But habit patterns disturbed, or seemingly shattered, by the explosion leave all kinds of rubble to be carried away or rearranged before genuine integration of life around Jesus matures.

That's why the church must fulfill the twin commands to preach and to teach. I'm happy for everyone who accepts Jesus. But I'm happier when by means of a powerful ministry in a congregation that new babe grows into maturity in Jesus.

On the Inside, Too

May 11, 1975

Most of us bear some easily detected resemblances to our parents. Did it ever occur to you that we look like our parents on the inside too? Our inner organs are like the ones our parents had, and we often become painfully aware of the fact that their weaknesses and ills are the ones to which we have fallen heir.

Doctors recognize this, and that's why they ask us, not only for a history of our diseases and illnesses, but of those of our parents as well.

I suppose we don't give much thought to how much we look like our heavenly Father on the outside, but we are agonizingly conscious of the fact that we ought to be like Him on the inside. Our sin and guilt and shame come from our failures to be on the inside what He has made us to be.

Often we rationalize, "We're only human!" No! We are more than that. We are His children. He has made us for himself. So when we look on the inside different from God in our thoughts, motives, and desires, we are confessing the problem of sin and temptation. The devil wants to make us look like himself outside and inside. Jesus came to help us to the wholeness and wholesomeness which is our true nature as God's children.

Should it be any wonder then that when people look at us in our moral, ethical, and theological nature they recognize that we are His children? Peter was recognized by his language as a Galilean. But his later life proved him to be the rock that Jesus said he would be.

We'll be recognized, too, by our language, our conduct, our love—all those qualities and expressions which show that on the inside we are like our Father.

Images of Joy

March 13, 1977

I've tried to think of ways to talk about joy and have usually felt defeated. One morning I found a poetic way to express my feelings about joy. So today, for the first time this column is poetry:

I start with pleasure
To get in touch with joy.
And pleasure is
The sun on me.
Fresh air to breathe and
The smell of pines.
The scurrying sounds of squirrels,
Bird songs and the lapping waters of a lake
At evening with a soft breeze stirring.
The smell of wood smoke from a campfire
And conversations with a friend,
Warm food on our table with the family,
The intriguing plot of a good book
Read on a cold winter evening in a quiet room.
The voices of children on Christmas morning,
A letter from a friend,
The swelling strains of music from a
Choir or organ or a symphony or a
Poem that crystallizes or shatters
Thoughts within the mind.

Pleasure is all these things and more and more.
But joy—that's knowing that every real pleasure
Is the work of God.
It's respect for life,
A celebration of living,
A praise for His hand in nature
And in you and me.
It's the guidance system in the soul
That, midst storm and strife, always points through
To the pole star of faith.

"So now abideth faith, hope, love."
But joy is the excitement and the fun,

The child at play in the kingdom of God.
So birds and squirrels
   Lakes and woodsmoke
      Friends and food and family
Are more, much more, than pleasure to me.
They are joy, because He has enlightened
My spirit by His Spirit
To perceive what mortal eye alone
   will always fail to see—

God comes close in all good things
And good things bring Him close to me.

Cosmetic Christianity

November 27, 1977

We've all heard and probably quoted the ancient judgment on beauty, "Beauty is only skin deep." Some wit added to that "But ugly goes all the way." How well we understand the truth of that in the moral and ethical realm. Evil penetrates life and distorts and destroys. Sin is not just a cosmetic on human behavior, therefore it cannot be successfully handled in external ways. There is no moral or ethical cosmetic kit on the market that will deal with sin in the human heart.

But we often try to deal with it that way. We cover our inner ugliness with external acts of self-righteousness. We draw attention to this self-righteousness by condemning evil in others. We profess loyalty to Jesus by hateful dogmatism. We think that hating evil around us is equal to loving God. Sometimes we demonstrate loyalty to church services, faithfulness in giving, and response to every call for work while failing totally to search our hearts in prayer and meditation on His word.

If there were only a cosmetic kit that would make us righteous, we'd buy it. But Jesus did not come to add to the window dressing and cosmetology that makes scribes and Pharisees. He labeled that approach to God hypocrisy.

He came that we might be changed in our hearts so that our outer deeds would be a profession of real life in Him, not a means to hide our twisted and sinful inner lives. That transforming work is never done. We are in a process of renewal day after day. Paul says that this renewal leads us into the knowledge of the one who created us according to his own likeness (Colossians 3:10).

Yes, the ugliness of sin goes all the way, but the power of His blood follows to cleanse and renew abundantly beyond every perversion of evil.

The More Subtle Humanism

June 25, 1978

What is humanism? Generally, we think of it as putting man in the very center of everything, especially in an intellectual sense. A Renaissance writer, Gianozzo Manetti, put it this way, "God may have created the world, but man transformed and improved it." A humanist, in the strictest sense of that word, puts God completely out and man completely into the picture of meaning. All meaning is in man.

There is a more subtle humanism, however, that tends to do this while still affirming God. Instead of stressing human intellect, this form of humanism makes all reality subject to human feelings. We see it in the current revival of religion that affirms validity on the basis of human experience: "I was healed, therefore I know the gospel is true." "I had this insight about what would happen when the rains returned again." "I just knew my sister would have twins." "I spoke in tongues."

If a man "knows" he's had an experience, no one can convince him otherwise. But what if he interprets such experiences as evidences of the gospel's truth or of special divine intervention? This replaces revelation with human sensation. It puts man at the center of meaning and nudges revelation aside.

Obviously, it is man who evaluates and accepts or rejects the record given in Scripture and therefore accepts or rejects Jesus and the salvation He brings. But that action should be based upon a confrontation with Scriptural facts rather than upon the fallibility of human experience and the equally fallible interpretations we make of such experiences.

Humanism may seem arrogant when it appears at the intellectual level, but it can be just as egotistical at the emotional level. Some are disposed toward a logical approach to Scripture and others favor an emotional or more experiential approach. Those in both groups need to beware of the danger of a man-centered religion. God's gracious seeking for us in Christ ought to keep us humble.

Car Wrecks Aren't the Only Way to Heaven

October 22, 1978

Twice today, cars with "Jesus" bumper stickers whizzed by me in traffic. One, an open sports car, weaved in and out of traffic until he almost caused a collision.

I was theorizing about this situation. Maybe there is a kind of Christian who just doesn't worry about wrecks at all. Maybe he expects the Lord to keep him safe (I've heard some say that), or maybe he expects to be caught up in the sky (there's a lot of talk about this), or maybe he just thinks "So what, if I die, I'll go to Heaven."

Well, the born-again drivers of those persuasions worry me. I'd sooner have people in cars who are a bit worried, too, people who realize that there is a mutual responsibility and courtesy generally expected of everyone who casts himself down behind the wheels of our lethal, legal monsters.

And I guess I'm not persuaded that the testimony the world needs is that Christians can drive as they please since they're on the way to Heaven. One guy buzzed right on by me the other night and he wasn't anywhere close to 55. His bumper testimony was "It's Fun Being a Christian."

Well, if you've gotten this far you probably feel as I do, or you've already gone out to soak the stickers off. Maybe someone is saying, "Oh come off it, George, don't you want to go to Heaven?" Yes I do, but I'd feel a bit embarrassed filling out the entrance form at the question: "You last resided where?" with "in a wrecked VW at the corner of Hillsdale and Foxworthy."

Seventy Times Seven

August 12, 1979

Almost anyone can recount some story about family members or acquaintances in which harbored resentment and an unforgiving spirit led to years of estrangement and separation. How often we hear, "Well, I'll not be the first to forgive" or "She doesn't deserve forgiveness" or "Why should I forgive him for such a thing as that?"

When Jesus counseled that we should forgive seventy times seven, He certainly was not suggesting that we keep records and quit at 490 times! The number of times is so great and the symbolic concept of perfection so strong in his formula, 70 x 7, that we can come to only one conclusion: Jesus teaches that forgiveness doesn't stop.

A young man spoke before Communion in the congregation where I shared this week. He pointed out that Jesus is always giving us "the second chance." With considerable emotion he gave his testimony to the encouragement that Christ's forgiveness brings. Over and over again, Jesus provides the cleansing for us when we sin. In Communion, in His memory, we are recalling His gift of death and life for each of us. He dealt with our sin. He is the greatest of all forgivers.

So why don't we quickly offer to others what we have received in such great abundance? If a man will lay down his life for a friend, why should he not quickly forgive him? We have only one life to give. But God has given and given and given us forgiveness. Freely we have received, freely we should give.

To be misers with forgiveness is to miss the heart of God. How many old wounds would heal, old estrangements be turned into fellowship, and burdens of guilt be lifted if we would just forgive others as He has forgiven us?

Forgiveness is not cheapened by abundance.

Manna Kept is Worms

August 26, 1979

God gave the manna to the children of Israel in the wilderness in response to their need and as a test of their obedience. They had complained to Moses of their hunger, so the Lord promised to "rain bread from heaven." The people were to gather each day's portion each day. This would test their ability to follow the Lord's instructions (Exodus 6:3, 4).

Shortly after this, contrary to the Lord's command, some people tried to store up some manna "and it bred worms and stank" (Exodus 16:20). By trusting the manna for food, instead of God, and by fearing that the food would run out, the blessing spoiled.

The manna of God's blessing today comes as a constant test of our ability to receive without being selfish. When we have the ability to accept the things God gives without trying to gorge on them, then we are free to really enjoy His blessings. But if we get caught up in the gifts themselves, trying to grasp and keep them, then we lose our sense of God. Before long everything is worms.

The manna also tests our faith. Can we believe that He will continue to provide? Do we even believe that He provides at all? There must have been Israelites who, having eaten manna from childhood as they grew up in the wilderness, took this marvelous gift as a natural phenomenon. It would be easy to believe that manna "just falls" every day, without seeing it as God's special provision.

When we lose our lives we find them. When we try to keep our lives we lose them.

Stealing Music

September 14, 1980

Did it ever occur to you while you were singing choruses out of a duplicated chorus booklet or praising God with a choir anthem from copied music that you could be using stolen music? Well, it's true. Often music that has been copied from one purchased copy in order to "save money for the Lord" is copyrighted material, and copying it is stealing.

The law is very specific on this. And the reason for the law is that the people who write, arrange, and publish earn their living by doing so. To copy copyrighted material of any kind is stealing. No rationalizations will change that fact.

Not long ago an article in a church journal advised that every church music department should examine its library and destroy all pirated material. Well, that's a route to protection before the law, but it is not a protection before the Lord. It's a legal remedy, but it does not care for the ethical problem.

The right way would be to go through the library, destroy all photocopied or mimeographed material, and then go out and purchase an equal number of copies to refill the library. Destruction of the copies protects the church from being caught. But purchase of copies to replace these makes restitution to those who have been wronged.

Even though this practice of copying copyrighted material is known to be widespread in churches, schools, and other organizations, the commonality of the sin cannot excuse the sinners. This practice is theft pure and simple. And just copying the words without the music is also prohibited by the law.

I sincerely hope that you who read this article will check to see if your congregation is involved. Certainly, with some the whole thing has come about in ignorance of the law. In any case, now is the time to obey the law and make restitution. If we all decide for honesty, a lot of copied material will go up in flames and purchases of music will sharply increase as the wrong is righted.

Can it really be any other way when Christians are involved?

Once Again About "Stolen Music"

November 9, 1980

Several weeks ago (September 14), I drew attention to the copyright law prohibiting the copying of sheet music. Some readers have called this article into question; mainly, I think, because of confusion between copying and performance regulations. I am not writing about performance. The practice I'm concerned about is the purchase of one piece of sheet music, and then copying it ten, twenty, or forty times.

The general scope of the copyright law is stated in Section 106: Five fundamental rights are given to copyright owners; "the exclusive rights of reproduction, adaptation, publication, performance, and display." These "bundle of rights" provide at length for various special situations, but prohibit the activity of copying as I have described it. The law also forbids the reproduction of words in song sheets or booklets.

For educational purposes the law provides for "emergency copying to replace copies that are not available for an imminent performance, provided purchased replacement copies shall be substituted in due course."

The intent of the law is further revealed in that "for academic purposes, other than performance, single copies of excerpts of works may be made, provided that the excerpts do not comprise a part of the whole which would constitute a performable unit...."

It is very plain that the law protects the copyright owner from having his material reproduced in ways other than ones authorized by him. As I emphasized in my previous article, this is the author's means of protection for his livelihood.

When we know that the law forbids the practice of copying, then doing so certainly constitutes stealing. The copyright owner alone has the right of reproduction. To disregard his right in order to save money takes money from his pocket. It is a practice that robs him of the fruit of his labor. The fact that we didn't use a gun, only a copy machine, doesn't make it any less a robbery.

CHAPTER SIX
SOCIAL ISSUES

This topic usually yields controversy, disagreement, and anxiety. George never shirked from his felt responsibility to offer comment and Christian perspective on any social issue. While none of us would likely agree with him on every issue, each of us can benefit from his common sense, stubborn logic, opinions, and Biblical insight brought to each column we have selected. Since they were first published, single issue politics has increasingly torn at the fabric of social cohesiveness in America—to the point that civility and reasoned dialog are too often supplanted by passion and mere rhetoric.

We suspect George could contribute significantly to the discussion of current social issues such as euthanasia, AIDS, affirmative action, and geriatric dilemmas. It may be possible to discern his views on current issues that vex us as we reread how he addressed key social policy flashpoints such as abortion, human rights, gun control, poverty, materialism, family life, and media. In his writings there is no patience with social withdrawal or with a cowering retreat into private peace and security. George urges us to engage and confront the social evils of our time with Christian prophetic responsibility even as we prioritize the gospel into all our activities and daily life.

Theory or Fact?

February 11, 1973

How did life originate on the earth? Creationists believe that God created life in the beginning. Noncreationists subscribe to the theory that at some moment billions of years ago the exact chemical constituents necessary for life accidentally got together and life began. After this, through a long evolutionary process, all life forms developed. Because of these divergent views there has been a serious contention in California (probably in other states as well) about how the origin of life should be taught in the public schools.

A recent decision by the California State Board of Education will affect science textbooks used in the schools. These books will now say that "many scientists believe that life may have begun in the sea." This decision marks a distinct victory for those who have contended that evolution is a theory of the development of life, not a fact about this development.

In all fairness, we must note that many creationists believe in evolution as the means of the development of life while they hold firmly to the belief that God created life and developed it. The essence of the problem has been the teaching that life started without God.

Of what importance will this decision be for the children in the schools of California? Most important, it seems to me, will be the fact that no longer will the noncreationist view be taught as fact in direct conflict to what every child from a Christian home has been taught. Children will not have to be either "religious" or "scientific." Now it will be recognized that one can be both. Many great scientists have proved this and are proving this today by devout discipleship to Jesus.

Respect for Life

February 25, 1973

Abraham Lincoln gave one of his most compelling arguments against slavery in the form of a question: "Is the slave a man?" To affirm that was to affirm the inherent wrongness of slavery. No rationalization could avoid the conclusion that slaves were men. Who has the right to own another man?

In the modern abortion controversy all kinds of rationalizations are put forth attempting to avoid the conclusion that abortion constitutes a violent destruction of life. This horrifying fact is usually obscured behind arguments about a woman's rights over her own body, or the sorrow that a crippled child might bring to himself or society, or the psychological damage to a woman forced to bear an unwanted child, etc.

What do all these arguments amount to? Not much, really. Not even an arbitrary medical definition as to when a fetus becomes a human can set aside the fact that human life begins as a fetus. What if we arbitrarily defined a human as one six months old. Would that justify the destruction of infants?

There are young women who will cry because some homeless kittens are "put to sleep" at the pound, who will righteously defend their right to abortion. Why, at this time when we hear so many pleas for the dignity of life, do we also hear a constant stream of argument claiming that a fetus is the personal property of the woman who carries it?

The answer is simple. When men look at this world as pagans and put God and His laws out of their minds, then they become their own lawmakers. Men then make laws for their own convenience. Pagans in ancient Rome put unwanted infants to death. Christians and Jews refused to do this and condemned the practice. Eventually Rome made the practice illegal.

The exceptional case where doctors cannot save both mother and child comes about just because medical skill has not advanced this far. Those who must make this decision will have to make it, but such a decision cannot provide an argument for abortion as a human right to be exercised under any and all circumstances.

Possibly one thing that God was teaching us in the birth of Jesus was a sanctuary for divine life. God is always in charge of this miracle of life. No rationalization can ever get around that.

What's Media?

March 11, 1973

I saw a cartoon in *World* magazine showing three medieval scribes copying the Bible. One is saying to the others, "What do you mean, 'What's media?' We're media." In the modern sense anyone or anything that transmits a message is media. Moses coming down from Sinai with the tablets of the law was media, and the tablets were, too. Moses had been with God, and he was delivering God's message to the people. God had used a burning bush or media to show Moses that he was on holy ground.

All the prophets were media. They did not invent messages. They spoke the messages God gave them. In the New Testament Jesus is media. John calls Him the Word, using the Greek word, *logos*, to express that Jesus came as God's message to us. He became our priest, our mediator, in all things pertaining to God because He was both God and man.

The four Gospels are the record of how Jesus brought the knowledge of God to man. Acts shows how He continued to do this through His church.

So who is media now? Paul says that Christians are "lights in the world, God's children in the midst of a crooked and perverse generation, holding forth the word of life" (Philippians 2:15, 16). You see, God could have kept on sending prophets, but He sent Jesus in flesh. This was a more powerful, more compelling way to reach man. So now He uses Christians, who are temples of the Holy Spirit, that the living message may go forth from dedicated lives.

His message is still clothed in flesh. We are redeemed, Peter says, "to proclaim the excellencies of Him who has called you out of darkness and into His marvelous light (1 Peter 2:9). So we don't have to copy the Bible by hand to be media now, but the world must see in us the person and power of Jesus. When that happens, we're media!

Humanism Is Too Human

November 25, 1973

Recently 120 members of the Humanist Society signed a document claiming that there can be no divine intervention in human affairs, and so man must solve all his problems by himself. They further claimed that religion had done a disservice to man by suggesting that man may look to God. Their contention is that this distracts man from self-actualization and from rectifying injustices.

Similar in content to *Humanist Manifesto I* published in 1933, this new document, *Humanist Manifesto II*, is directed to the problems of our age. Many of the goals set forth by these scientists, literary people, social scientists, and others are worthy. Who doesn't want to be rid of war? Wouldn't the world be better if social justice prevailed? How wonderful if all men could enjoy a truly open and democratic society.

Now there's the rub. The Humanist Society wants to achieve these goals with the raw material of unredeemed man. "We affirm," they say, "that morality and ethics (if such could even exist) would have to come from man. Christians believe, however, that God has adequately revealed himself and His will for man. And, second, we believe that moral and ethical systems based solely on humanly devised values have been exposed again and again as falling short in giving mankind happiness and the good life."

It isn't that man has believed in God and His revealed will that has caused the problems. It's that he has believed too little and disobeyed God too much.

Humanly devised ethical systems are based on fallible man. What would the Humanist Society think if the majority of the world's people should decide to kill off all Caucasian people? Who could call that wrong on the basis of human value assessments? After all, the majority would be acting out their convictions!

And that's the trouble with all human systems of value. They are just too human.

The Crucible

December 8, 1974

A congressional committee recently warned that almost five hundred million people in the world are desperately hungry. The committee predicted that ten million of these hungry people, mostly children, will die in the next several months. That brings upon our society an ethical test of major importance. How do we accept our stewardship of a tremendous productivity in food? And how will we change our habit of a very wasteful use of food?

We eat a super-abundant amount of meat in the United States. General dietary requirements call for no more than four ounces of meat a day. Many people get their protein in other ways. Yet Americans often indulge in steak dinners in an almost completely gluttonous manner. Cattle eating grain products are very inefficient producers of food for man. An acre of ground in cereal grains will feed about ten times as many people as that acre devoted to feeding meat animals.

Will we, during the next few decades, see our food producing capacity as a public trust for people everywhere in the same way that we'd like to see the Arab nations view their oil reserves as a public trust? Will we see this issue seriously enough to lighten our demands for oil and also use our land in the most productive ways we can to feed hungry people while we aid them to control population and produce more food?

We are in the greatest testing time in the history of the world. The years ahead will determine whether ethical, moral, and spiritual sensitivity will be strong enough to offset selfishness, greed, luxury and waste. President Ford has asked for a beginning in sacrifice, hard work, and conservation. We'd better give heed. The world is in the crucible.

The Pervasive Influence

January 4, 1976

Many of us can remember when there was no television, but now a whole generation has been raised where it has been almost impossible to get away from the picture tube. Some intellectually oriented people seem to show a kind of guilt about this influence. I hear remarks like "I happened to see a part of—the other night," or "My wife was watching," or "I seldom see movies on television, but—" Why the guilt? What judgments are we making about this pervasive medium when we talk this way?

Certainly we recognize that moral values held by Christians are regularly trampled in television programs. I just happened to see a part of a variety show the other day where the central actors were chimpanzees all very primly dressed in human clothes—almost completely covered. That was sort of cute—chimpanzees in clothes, not naked as we usually see them. But the woman attendant with the chimps wasn't dressed nearly as much as the chimps. So here was a mixture: nice clean American circus, family entertainment, and nightclub exhibitionism all in one package.

You just can't view television very long on any given day without hearing language that would have brought a licking when some of us were kids. Besides this, the soap-opera imitation of life, the crime-oriented approach to human problems, the prize-in-every-pot game shows with screaming, crying, emoting contestants gathering in the loot—all these make one wonder if this media may not just be a means to dissipate a great amount of time with little or no value in return.

There are good programs. This is granted. Educational television is doing some great things. Some excellent drama is shown, some fine music, etc. But we'll all be guilty if we do not exercise some genuine discernment. Television has a way of bringing the theatre, the street, the magazine rack, the newspapers, the nightclubs, the bars, just about everything right into our homes. That little off-on switch is our invitation or our refusal to a multitude of guest.

I just happened to see some things lately that made me think of this.

Who Pulled the Plug?

January 11, 1976

Recently in New Jersey the law has asserted that no one—parents, doctors, or the government—has the right to remove the plug that keeps life-support equipment in operation for a young woman who has ceased to have any possibility of normal life again. In another case someone removed the plug, and the law is seeking that person.

Are we to be victimized by our machines so that regardless of cost we must pay subservience to them? Already over a hundred thousand dollars have been spent in one of these cases, and across the land similar exorbitant expense is put forth for people who haven't the power to make a decision for themselves.

Strange, isn't it? While we do this in support of our ideal that the right to live is inalienable, we also pass laws that make it legal to destroy the unborn, contending that women must have a right to decide whether they want to be mothers.

And is it not strange that while we bring whole surgical teams at immense expense to the aid of some people in our society, millions of others here and throughout the world never have the benefit of a doctor? While hundreds of thousands of dollars go out in vain efforts for one, thousands of children in Africa, India, the United States, and other places go without medical help and without sufficient nourishment.

As the air becomes more unbreathable, the seas and waterways more polluted, so that life for all is threatened, isn't it strange that we do not cry out in alarm that someone is pulling the plug on our life-support systems?

Perhaps it's time to break our fascination with exotic scientific equipment and focus again on people. That's what made Jesus so different from others in His world. While leaders were obsessed with religious forms, neat theological explanations, and public display of sanctity, Jesus came and loved people. He plugged us into life. It's time to get fascinated with that.

What About Infanticide?

May 16, 1976

She sat down. Her speech was finished. She'd just given the regular arguments defending abortion. Among them was this: "No mother should have to carry to birth a baby which might be deformed." She was a student in a speech class in a large state university. I was the teacher. Now it was time for discussion.

I commented on her organization, manner of delivery, and a few other items. Then I told the class that I had what I thought was a better solution. "Why not let every conception go full term? Then after birth, have physicians and psychiatrists make examinations and tests over a period of six months to determine whether the child is healthy and mentally proficient, with prospects of a productive life. If not, then it could be destroyed and we wouldn't run the risk of destroying infants before birth that we should have saved."

The class was horrified and indignant. They couldn't imagine such a crass, inhuman way of dealing with babies. This forced into the open a discussion of who is to make the decision about who is alive and who is a person. Some of the students began to see that they had accepted without question somebody else's idea that there isn't a real person until the twenty-fourth or the twenty-eighth week, or some other time set arbitrarily. Who says so? How do we know that's true? Does the Supreme Court or a council of physicians have the right to determine this?

Yes, they would have that right if there were no God, no Heaven, and no eternal spirit to man. If we are willing to accept that kind of world, wouldn't my non-abortion infanticide view be more practical?

We'd better start asserting that we want none of that!

When the Guns Are Silent

November 12, 1978

When the guns are silent and the burial details have finished their grim work, hospitals are filled with broken pieces and neatly dressed diplomats argue the results across treaty tables, relaxing together with expensive cigars and cocktails. Then the little people of the world ask, "Why?" Widows, fatherless children, and weeping mothers and fathers ask, "Why?"

Regardless of the efforts made to justify any war, that "why," cannot be answered. Wars aren't holy. Wars don't end wars. Wars are not an expression of popular morality. Wars don't settle anything for long. President Eisenhower condemned war: "When people speak to you about a preventive war, you tell them to go and fight it. After my experience, I have come to hate war. War settles nothing." And even if we must argue with the definition that equates war with Hell, we certainly can't find war's source in Heaven.

The real answer to that "why" is simple. Sin brings war. Human pride, selfishness, hatred are all involved, and sin is the root of it all. All the wreckage of war is a monument to the abysmal wickedness of man. Men start wars for personal gain, for power, even for pleasure. Patton's chilling evaluation of war in the movie "Patton" frightens us. He said, "I love it."

I am frightened, too, when I hear Christians suggest preventive war, or war to save the world for evangelism. Let's admit that war comes from a failure in men. We may be powerless to prevent wars now, but we certainly are not powerless to work for peace. The church's mission is to take the gospel to everyone in the world. That's the only real alternative to war. We live now in the relative quiet of an uneasy world peace. Let's redeem this time to vigorously pour our efforts into reaching this world for Christ. History has shown that the guns don't remain silent for long.

Equal Opportunity

October 14, 1979

I grew up in a poor family with no history of anyone ever getting a college education. (The only one who came close was Aunt Martha, who was a nurse and was held up to my brother and sister and me as an example of getting ahead.) But even after my folks went completely broke in the depression and lost all our farm animals and machinery, we still retained the vision, the American dream, that anyone can get ahead if he wants to.

Most of us can cite examples of this dream coming true, either from experience or from the accounts of great men such as Lincoln or Carnegie. But these examples are only exceptions. The facts do not bear out that this kind of opportunity, equal opportunity, really exists.

A 1972 study published by the Carnegie Commission reveals some hard facts about the plight of the poor. This report shows that two children of equal ability from two families of unequal income do not have equal futures. Suppose that the first child has a father with a $35,000 annual salary and that the second child's father earns only $4,800. It is twenty-seven times more likely that the child of the prosperous parent will get a job that puts him in the top tenth of national incomes. The child of the poor father has only about one chance in eight of earning even a median income.

Since people concerned about such injustice have generally been influenced by the American dream concept, most programs have concentrated on helping children as they grow up. Little attention has been given to equalizing opportunities in their futures.

We Christians must be concerned about the conditions of injustice prevailing in our society. It is all too easy to accept the common national myths, join forces with those who claim that we need harsher laws to protect property rights, and concentrate our attention on the eradication of a few of the more gross and obvious sins. If we isolate ourselves from the realities of the culture around us, we will have a hard time convincing others that we believe in a God who loves.

Are you convinced that He loves *everyone*?

Gun Control

April 13, 1980

My father traded off his thirty-eight caliber Colt revolver for a twenty-two Remington (model 12A) rifle for me when I was twelve years old. Before that I had a BB gun and had become a dedicated sparrow hunter around our farm. The Remington opened up a whole new range of destructive possibilities for me. The BB gun was too weak against crows and magpies. Actually, it took a very good shot to bring a sparrow down with it. I really didn't kill very many sparrows.

But the twenty-two was a real weapon. The day I bagged a big pheasant rooster at the edge of our garden by the poplar grove my mother was ecstatic. I'd put meat on the table. That was special.

I took great care of that rifle, cleaning it after every hunt, rubbing oil into the polished walnut stock and forearm. And my father taught me to be careful: "Keep the chamber empty; keep the safety on; don't point a gun at anything you don't intend to shoot." Cryptic rules. I heeded them.

Then I took the rifle with me on a mountain trip with two friends. My father hauled us to the head of the trail and said goodbye, and we were on our own. We carried everything on our backs. We didn't have the super lightweight gear that backpackers use today. It was a hard hike to the little valley, Buck Meadows, where we set up our camp. It was here that I learned about my gun. A chipmunk on a pine tree became my target. He dropped to the base of the tree with my shot, and I went over to the tree to get my prize. The bullet had split him open, exposing his little heart pumping frantically in the last moments of death.

I was stunned. Why had I killed him? What purpose was served? I was a visitor in his territory. I had become a dangerous invading force. Sure, I can't really remember exactly how sophisticated my views were then. I do know, however, that I grew up a lot that day. I moved from self-centered exploitation of life to a much more sensitive awareness of my role as a steward. That little chipmunk's heart introduced me to the mystery and value of life, to my own ignorant cruelty, and to responsibility.

He didn't die in vain. That day I learned gun control.

The Itch for More

July 27, 1980

He was fabulously rich and was being questioned on a TV interview program. "How much more must you get in order to be happy?" inquired the emcee.

The answer: "Always more."

Not long ago a fine Christian couple confessed, "We've gotten everything we need to enjoy life, but we are so busy still getting that we can't enjoy anything."

It's easy to get caught up in acquisition. In fact, we live in a society that makes acquisition an important value. If you don't own anything, then you aren't worth anything. Contrariwise, if you own a lot, you are valuable. And this can be ruinous. The Masai people in Africa have destroyed their own habitat, grazing lands, by not only building a livelihood from cattle but building a wealth system based on cattle. The more cattle a Masai has, the more valuable and important he is.

Paul lists this itch for acquisition among the grossest sins of the Gentiles (Romans 1:28-32). Along with evil, villainy, envy, murder, strife, and deceit, he names "covetousness," the lust to get. The Greek word was described by Greeks themselves to mean "the accursed love of having." It is the attitude that seeks for more and more.

Irritated by this itch, we seek for more things materially. We strive to be better than others and are caught up in our ambitions. We seek pleasure in life without regard for real needs or for the damage done to others. The itch for more is an irritation that knows no law and regards nothing but the need to keep getting more.

Jesus warned us about this, "Beware, stay on guard against the itch for more, because your life does not consist of the abundance of your possessions" (Luke 12:15, author's translation). Unless we heed this warning, we can easily get caught up in making a virtue out of what Jesus warned us was a vice.

Equality Under the Law

August 10, 1980

"Equality under the law shall not be denied or abridged by the United States or by any state on account of sex." That's the Equal Rights Amendment commonly called ERA. And what a battle it has generated! I suppose there will always be battles whenever the attempt is made to reduce prejudicial treatment of any group.

My first experience with this came early in my life. I was fifteen years old. I got a job on a farm and was put to work with a man. The job we did was easily measurable. I did just as much as he did, but I got paid less because I was a boy. That rankled me: the gross unfairness of it burned into me. Just as intolerable was the fact that for so long women could not vote in our democracy. And it took a Constitutional amendment to guarantee that black citizens could go to the polls without prejudicial registration tests.

In the controversy over the ERA, you can hardly find anyone who will say "I believe that sex should be a basis for non-equal treatment under the law," but it is not hard to find opponents of this amendment that positively affirms equality under the law.

Why is this? There are undoubtedly many reasons. But it is common in such disputes to hear many arguments that have no real bearing on the case at all. For example, it is argued "the ERA will destroy the home." How can this be? Would one actually argue that the integrity of the home depends upon a judicial system that denies or abridges rights under the law on the basis of sex? Are we looking for a scapegoat to carry the blame for the problems we are having with the home today?

ERA or no ERA, the Biblical teaching stands as the moral and spiritual law for Christians. The integrity of the home is established on a higher law than any made by man upon this earth.

The furor over ratification of this amendment has again drawn attention to the fact that there is always some distance between our profession of democracy and our practice of it. There is always resistance to establishing a government of, for, and by the people. Democracy is a whole lot easier to talk about than to practice. The theory of democracy is revered, the practice of it resisted.

The struggle for practical democracy is always a threat to entrenched authorities, special powers, privileges, and economic advantages. If there were presently no abridgments or denials of equality under the law on the basis of sex, it isn't very likely that some states would still be battling over ratification of the ERA.

What About the Poor?

May 17, 1981

We are in a period of national belt-tightening. According to the new administration in Washington, everyone has to share in this. The future of the whole country is now at stake, we are told, so everyone must feel the pinch, and sacrifices must be made. But while we are in this mood it is important that we do not lose our sense of compassion and sharing. Jumping on the bandwagon for sacrifice is not too difficult if the sacrifices don't hurt too much. It's a whole lot easier on the chicken than it is on the pig when they decide to sacrifice for a plate of ham and eggs. Those who give up a third car, or a second car, or meat once a week, or lower the thermostat a degree or two can easily forget that there are others that have no way to make these "sacrifices."

The poor often have no car, eat meat seldom, if at all, and at times cannot even pay for heat in the winter—never for air-conditioning in the summer. Amos thundered at the wealthy in his time for their luxuries, their insensitivity, and their plunder of the poor. He scorched the women: "Hear this word, you cows of Bashan who are on the mountain of Samaria, who oppress the poor, who crush the needy..." (Amos 4:1*). And he speaks for the Lord against the whole nation of Israel as well: "For three transgressions of Israel and for four I will not revoke its punishment, because they sell the righteous for money and the needy for a pair of sandals" (Amos 2:6).

He berates the people for the luxury of their summer and winter houses, for their gourmet eating habits and their costly ointments and wines.

So what does this say to us about the poor? Well, it surely says that God is concerned for the poor and He is concerned also for those who are wealthy that they do not misuse their wealth and the power that it gives.

A democratic society is not based on the idea that everyone has the same abilities, opportunities, and economic or political clout. But this does not imply a survival-of-the-fittest idea. We are not living under license to get and keep all we can without regard for others. We do not have the right to impoverish others for our gain.

As we tighten the national belt and learn how to live within our means, we must not allow the burdens for the sacrifices to fall too heavily on those who can least afford to give up anything they have.

The poor are already hurting. They will hurt even more in the wake of our austerity programs. Christians must be aware of the suffering and anguish felt by others for the bare necessities of life. In our communities we can exhibit the compassion of our Lord by direct action to help those who are in need both within and outside the church. Perhaps the greatest influence we can have for the gospel is simply to live and share as Jesus taught us to do.

----

*Scripture quotes are from the *New American Standard Bible*.

We've Come a Long Way

September 20, 1981

It is refreshing to find President Reagan announcing Sandra O'Connor as his choice for Supreme Court justice. In this act he has broken a two-hundred-year-old precedent that saw only men serving on the high bench.

His action symbolizes that women have come more fully into the intellectual and political mainstream in America than ever before. It took over half a century of vigorous effort by women just to get the vote, even though our constitution said nothing about forbidding them this citizens' right. Now, at last, two branches of our government will be represented by women (presuming, of course, Mrs. O'Connor's ratification by the Senate). Will we someday see a woman in the presidency?

When a new justice is appointed, many voices are heard clamoring for someone to "balance the court," to support so-called "conservative" or "liberal" positions, or to be dedicated to some particular special interest of the time.

What seems much more important to me is that the appointee be a dedicated, competent jurist concerned with justice. Presumably, Sandra O'Connor will be on the bench for many years, spanning several administrations, changes of party control, and in times when new issues constantly come before the public and the court. She and the other justices will have to make decisions on a whole range of problems inherent in our rapidly changing world. What we need from the court is a sensitivity to the principles of the constitution and a commitment to the preservation of human rights as they are guaranteed in that document.

Ours is a world where men make decisions about war, where men generally determine the economic trends, in short, where men operate at all the high levels of decision making. Sandra O'Connor's appointment is a hopeful sign that a woman's voice will be heard in decisions bearing on the great constitutional problems surfacing in a troubled America.

Is It One World?

March 21, 1982

As I write this article, the summit conference of rich and poor nations is under way in Mexico. Predictably, the perceptions of these leaders about world issues vary greatly. After all, a nation with an annual average income of two hundred dollars will be operating out of needs very different from a nation like our own, the richest nation in the world.

Basically, the rich nations are not at all anxious to limit their prosperity or to share it with poorer nations, just as rich people within a country usually do not exhibit an overwhelming compulsion to share what they have with the poor. And this can be very frustrating for those nations who supply many basic raw materials to rich nations, only then to become a part of the market for manufactured goods coming out of those same rich nations. Simply to tell these poor nations to industrialize may be to ask the impossible in view of the established competition.

Here in our own country, small firms and small farms are dying because there is no way for the little fellow to compete with the super farms and the super industrial conglomerates. Here in the Northwest where I live, it is becoming virtually impossible for the small lumbering firms to meet the competition from the big firms.

Sensitivity to the plight of the poor nations is absolutely essential if we are to realize a community of nations on this globe. Some sacrifices for their help must certainly be made.

Our own American assumption that we are the great give-away nation needs to be set straight so that we do not act callously toward poor countries. For example, Ron Sider, in his book, *Rich Christians in an Age of Hunger*, quotes a statistic that stands out for me. In 1975, *The World Book*'s estimates on official development assistance from industrialized countries to poor countries as a percentage of gross national product showed us, the United States, thirteenth down the list. We gave about one-fourth of one percent of our gross national product in foreign aid. This was out of a list of seventeen industrialized nations. In view of the trade we have with poor countries, it may be that we reap more than we give. Maybe we aren't giving away anything at all.

The tremendous disparity between the rich and the poor is a dangerous and threatening problem. We surely are not near any kind of international or world government. But we all live in one world, like it or not.

A Television World

August 15, 1982

A thirty-second TV commercial during the Super Bowl football game cost $340,000. For that money the advertiser could expect to get his message to about 105 million people! That figures out to about one-third of a penny for each person. So it's a whole lot cheaper, even at $340,000, than stamps or envelopes or telephone calls.

The fact that advertisers will spend such sums is just another proof that ours is a television world. In a lifetime, an average American will invest 50,000 to 75,000 hours in watching TV. That kind of investment and exposure must have some effect on thinking, on values, and on moral and ethical conduct.

Some who have attempted to evaluate the effect of TV on our lives have suggested that it isn't just an immoral program or bad language or violence that should concern us. We need to be concerned for the totality of the effect of TV's point of view. TV gives us a picture world, not reality. Many problems, even complex ones, are developed and solved in thirty minutes or in an hour or two. Life isn't that simple The news comes to us in short clips edited out of much more footage and arranged to present the concept of what happened that fits the opinion of the news agency. Of even more concern to Christians is TV's focus and emphasis. God doesn't play much of a part in the world of TV. We are led to put our attention on the sports stars, the actors, the comedians. In short, TV presents a world view with man at the center of everything.

This fall's political campaigns will give us a massive dose of media pitches by politicians. Issues aren't so important; personalities are. Even when the issues are presented, they will be generally oversimplified and often distorted. We will be led to think that there are only two sides to the complex problems of the times. Candidates will be "sold" to us by brief quotations, cute little scenes with families, at a fair, or on someone's farm.

So what can we do about this? Be wary. Just because it's on TV doesn't mean that it's true or real or accurate. *TV Guide* recently asserted that an "in-depth" news analysis had terribly distorted the facts involved. That may be much more common than we think. Be wary.

Somewhat facetiously, Will Rogers said, "All I know is what I read in the papers." We had better be careful that all we know does *not* come from television. We dare not intemperately park ourselves in front of the TV set to gain our ultimate understanding of our lives and of our world.

When There Are No 'Acts of God'

May 19, 1985

I asked a missionary doctor way out in the bush in Rhodesia (now Zimbabwe) how his African patients reacted to medical treatment that fails. In my mind were pictures of reprisal against the foreigner who harmed a child, killed a wife in childbirth, or destroyed a family member in surgery. My friend set me straight, "When there is failure, when loved ones die, the Africans say, 'It was God's will.' That's all there is to it."

Today I thought about that again as I read my morning paper. One article in particular concerned me. Many obstetricians, so the article said, are becoming gynecologists, no longer delivering babies as a part of their practice. Why? Because lawsuits against them have become so frequent and for such great amounts that their insurance costs against malpractice have skyrocketed. Besides this, the trauma of being sued and held responsible for an infant death or deformity is more than many of these doctors want to bear.

Why are doctors being sued so much now? Let's admit that there are some legitimate claims against doctors who have failed to be professional. But that doesn't account for this rash of suits that plagues the obstetricians. Behind much of this seems to be the idea that we are in a scientific world where everything should be controllable. If things go badly, we aren't likely to say, "It was God's will"; we are more likely to ask, "Who goofed up? Who made the mistake?"

Surely it isn't fair to assign all kinds of bad things to God as "acts of God." But we can recognize that not everything is an act of man, either, that man is not in supreme control of life and death.

When we become so arrogant that nothing for us is an "act of God," then we descend to the level of faultfinders, trying to make someone pay for everything that goes wrong. We will put medical aid out of reach financially for many if we persist in this.

CHAPTER SEVEN

GOVERNMENT-THE NATION

While he never taught a college course in American Government or Political Science, no student ever left a George Alder class bereft of instruction and perspective regarding politics and government. He didn't politicize classes but ensured that students connected to the larger world of power, structure, laws, and political process. In a world where it is presumed conservative Christians are automatically Republicans, it could come as quite a shock to learn that George was a Democrat. He was appalled that any would think him to be anti-American, soft on Communism, or subversive. He was accused of all three at least once in his life. George Alder was defined by his faith, not his politics—aligning and realigning himself with parties, candidates and causes that best promoted his Christian conviction that our world could become more fair and humane, reflecting God's care and justice. He realized that much of politics is a matter of opinion and that sincere Christians equally committed to Christ and His mission can disagree with integrity. At the dawn of a new millennium, the articles that follow seem more tame and even conservative than when first penned. Yet they still carry compelling rationale—enough for us each to pause and reflect once again, if not for the first time.

Voting Time

November 5, 1972

It's voting time again. A fantastic amount of human suffering, sacrifice, and work has gone into providing the democratic process and the ballot box. Yet at election time many are tempted to cut the whole system down with "What difference will it make?" or "I'm a citizen of heaven, so why should I be concerned about worldly governments? They're all doomed anyway."

It is true that Paul said "we are citizens of heaven" (Philippians 3:20), but he also argued for responsible earthly citizenship in Romans 13, and he held his own Roman citizenship of real value. Jesus said that we should give Caesar his due, and He didn't add that we should do that grudgingly. Christians have a responsibility to heaven and to earth.

Election time can be a time when we measure how we feel about this dual citizenship. Some Christians get so frustrated trying to understand the candidates and the issues that they just give up, refusing to vote at all, or, if voting, they do it in a perfunctory manner. Others get so involved that they forget that God's whole concern may not be that their favorite candidate win. They may also forget that doomsday has a surprising and persistent way of refusing to come on the day after election.

Some parents this year will be disturbed to find that their newly qualified eighteen-year-olds will not agree with them on the issues or the candidates. Some eighteen-year-olds will marvel at their parents' lack of understanding about local and national politics.

I'm not suggesting that there is no real difference in parties or candidates, or that it doesn't make any difference how we vote. But I am convinced that God is not solely on one side or the other. The important thing is to go to the polls seriously and prayerfully, and to vote as a responsible citizen of the United States and of the kingdom of heaven.

If Daniel Came Today

May 12, 1974

Would we be comfortable if Daniel should come to America? God used him long ago to warn great world leaders, Nebuchadnezzar and Belshazzar, that human temples of pride and power cannot stand. These two kings were powerful, proud men. They thought that by their power they had established their reigns. Daniel told them that God was not pleased with their proud, arrogant ways. God said that they were heading for a fall. And they fell.

If Daniel should come to the United States would he compliment us for our technocracy, our space travel, our military might, and our superior living standard? Would he say, "God is proud of you, America, because you are number one among nations"? Would he say, "You are great because you use up fifty percent of the world's energy to bring comfort to six percent of the world's people"? Would he compliment us on our national achievements and on our national pride? Would he say, "You know God loves you best because you are the richest nation on earth"?

Have we gotten so caught in your pride that we believe that, although God judged other nations *for* pride, He is blessing us *in* our pride? Have we been unwittingly wiring a destructive mechanism into our national life through our selfishness, sinfulness, and haughtiness? Are we so dedicated to slogans and unrealistic evaluation of ourselves that like Nebuchadnezzar and Belshazzar we have pushed God to the borders of our thinking?

In personal life and in national life pride precedes destruction. Humility counters pride and brings submission to God and repentance of sins. How tangled in this web of national pride have we Christians become? We would be happy to hear a Daniel only if we have turned from our pride and humbled ourselves before God. Unless we humble ourselves, repent of our sins and pray, we may well hear "Thou are weighed in the balances, and art found wanting" (Daniel 5:27)!

One Man, One Vote

October 31, 1976

It's difficult to do God's will on earth in any but a very imperfect way. This is true personally and especially in political and social ways. On a world scale we have so far found it impossible. Even our idea of representative government as a recognition of fundamental rights has been difficult to implement here and almost impossible to export to others.

The idea that every person has a right to vote is based on a revolutionary idea of two hundred years ago. "All men are created equal." That idea is Biblical. But to implement this fundamental concept at the ballot box has been a long and difficult struggle. Why was it that in the beginning mainly white-property-owning males were at the boxes? Why so long before women could go there? Why for so long could we ask teenagers to die in battle while we could not trust them to vote about the policies that sent them there? Why have we had to pass voting rights laws even after a constitutional amendment guarantees them?

The equality idea is an ideal. To live by it, to implement it is difficult for sinful men. So going into that ballot box may seem a common right to us. The majority of the people of the world have never enjoyed that right. Equality is not even held as an ideal in most of the world.

"One man, one vote" says a lot about how we look at ourselves and others. To the degree that we really let people go to the boxes, we express our trust in "all men are created equal." To the degree that we keep them away, we express our distrust and a desire to maintain control. Voting is rather awesome, isn't it?

Romans 13 and Revelation 13

January 9, 1977

Civil government is essential and can often be a blessing to a society. Paul makes it clear in Romans 13 that Christians must respect civil government and that the government is not to be feared by the law-abiding citizen. The government he was talking about particularly was the Roman dictatorship under the Caesars.

However, before that century was over the Roman government was persecuting Christians who refused to conform to its demands. What had happened? How had the picture of a beneficent government become the picture of a ravenous beast as pictured in Revelation 13?

Roman Caesars tried to make religion the tool of the state to heal the divisions in the empire. A unified, conforming religious view that accepted a deified emperor was their solution. But Christians could not accept the emperor as God or even as a god. So the government tried to force that conformity. Thousands and thousands of Christians died in the terrible persecutions that followed.

The warning is clear. Civil government should be just that. It should not try to take over the functions of God in the society. Nor should Christians uncritically accept all the pronouncements of government, as if those pronouncements were God's will. God wills that government exist, but He does not will nor approve all that governments do.

When governments get proud and powerful the distance between Romans 13 and Revelation 13 can be traveled very quickly.

So What's Wrong With Heroes?

February 18, 1979

This is the month for national heroes. Lincoln and Washington are remembered this month as men who came to the front as outstanding leaders during crisis periods in our history. The heroes of a society usually represent the qualities of life that the people in that society admire. Our heroes live out for us the kind of character, conviction, and performance that we long for, even if we do not always achieve it.

Since heroes are humans, too, it is not so very difficult to find human weaknesses in them. All men are sinners, so why should we be terribly surprised to discover some hidden weakness in one of our heroes? Yet some people seem dedicated to finding every flaw, every error, every unsavory incident in the lives of heroes. What does this accomplish? Well, if no man can be admired, no woman held up as a model of virtue, and no religious person looked to as an example of faith—how will the standards for a society be modeled?

Those who destroy the heroes usually do not take their places or find anyone else to take their places, either. Youth and adults alike need the heroes' examples, whether they are heroes from the Bible or from the national life.

Lincoln and Washington represent honesty, hard work, dedication, respect for others, love of country, reverence for God, and personal sacrifice. Surely, their sins can also be found out, but that only proves that good qualities can outnumber and outweigh base and evil ones.

When it becomes fashionable always to find the evil and disregard the good, a society will move toward evil and not toward good. It is both Christian and humanly sound to think on those things that are "true... honest... just... pure... lovely... of good report" (Philippians 4:8). When we find these qualities in our heroes, then we will find them in ourselves. A society without heroes has the deepest poverty of all.

To Keep a Dream Alive

June 29, 1980

Freedom—what a dream! And what a price men have paid for that dream. Think of the sacrifices in families where dads and sons and husbands never came home, or where they came home with empty sleeves and trouser legs, blinded, maimed, and broken.

It takes something special to keep this dream alive. And it seems today that somehow the dream has dimmed.

The ballot boxes are still open, but a lot of folks stay home, and the flag goes by and they don't stand anymore, and only a few remember the words of the national anthem.

In many countries, leaders try to extinguish the dream. All over the world the enemies of freedom abound, and they mock the word while putting those who disagree into prisons, labor camps, or graves. And their dreamers flee away in rotten boats, hack their way through barbed-wire barriers, or contrive elaborate escape plans to leave their prison-paradise for a free land.

Let's lift up our heads. We may have a lot to be ashamed of and a lot for which to seek forgiveness. But remember, we don't have to escape this country to find freedom. We never need apologize for the dream. There's nothing wrong with the tears that wet the cheek when the flag goes by, and it's a lot more than sentimentalism that takes us to the ballot box and swells our voices in singing, "Oh, say can you see . . . ."

So on Friday all across the land the parades will pass, and we'll eat the hot dogs at our picnics, and we'll "ooh" and "aah" at the fireworks in the evening at the fairgrounds. That's not enough to keep the dream alive. But the way to kill the dream is to sit at home, lament the sad state of affairs, and maintain a lofty cynicism about patriotism, democracy, loyalty, and freedom.

It's better by far to share in the celebration of the dream than to be a part of that merciless conspiracy that would put it to death. You know and I know that we must keep the dream alive. If we don't, who will?

Your Vote Is Precious

October 19, 1980

What if someone had an election and no one came? Well, a party without guests is a failure and an election without voters is a farce. It is also a farce if those who vote can only affirm, having no real choice presented to them.

Our democratic system is being challenged now, not only from outside but from inside. The millions who do not vote exercise a quiet subversion to the system. Why don't they vote? Let me hazard some guesses.

The democratic process requires some faith that what citizens want they can get by voting. The system is based upon the idea that government is of, for, and by the *people*. When people feel that government is unresponsive, self-serving, and powerful enough to ignore the cries of the voters, then disillusionment sets in.

Today the media constantly carries stories of citizens battling the government and usually losing. The bureaucracy is so massive and powerful as to dwarf the efforts of protest from any one citizen. Many citizens do not visualize government as primarily interested in serving people, but much more as separate from and an adversary to people. These negatives are probably exaggerated (negatives usually are), but these attitudes do exist, and they keep voters away. People quit participating if they visualize participation as useless.

If we should come to a point where only a minority of all eligible voters go to the polls, then we would be on our way to the exercise of power by a smaller and smaller part of the body politic. Democracy dies unless we participate. And it does if it is ineffective in coping with the real problems of our real world.

Only an informed citizenry diligent at the polls and relentless in demanding responsibility from elected officials can make democracy work. It's easy to find cynics and critics of our system. We need citizens who are citizens indeed. Neglecting the ballot box drives a nail in the coffin that holds the remains of many attempts to make this democratic ideal a reality.

Under God

March 1, 1981

Yesterday (January 20) we watched the brief, orderly, entirely peaceful ceremony of the transfer of power from one presidential administration to another. At one instant in time President Carter became ex-president as President-elect Ronald Reagan became president. It was as simple as that. The ceremony was not forced upon these men. There were no soldiers there with guns trained upon them. The deposed did not hear "Off with his head!" In fact, President Carter had already accepted an appointment as special envoy for the new president to greet our fifty-two fellow Americans returning from their unlawful imprisonment in a foreign country.

Certainly, we all take this pretty much for granted. After all, we are Americans and this is America. We vote for our leaders; we don't shoot them out of power or violently bring them into power. Nevertheless, yesterday the release of our fellow citizens underscored the tremendous blessings we enjoy in this country under this form of government. We were reminded to remember that "under God" is not an empty phrase.

From ancient times it has been a part of international relationships to honor and protect the diplomatic representatives of other nations. Traditionally, these persons have been held almost in reverence as inviolate; to do them any harm at all has been viewed as the act of irresponsible barbarians.

How can nations keep in contact, do business, and resolve differences without mediators? And if these mediators are to be held personally responsible for the wrongs or imagined wrongs of their governments, then there can be no serious or responsible communications between world powers.

When governments are confused and divided internally, and when power is uncertain, then serious consequences follow. Unfortunately, the distressed people of Iran have been deeply alienated from the family of nations by these violations of custom and human decency.

Now that our people are home, we must resist the low impulse to revenge. Nothing worthwhile is ever accomplished by trying to take the right of revenge from God to ourselves. The militants in Iran held a small group of Americans hostage to embarrass us. Why should we accept that embarrassment and add to it by walking their same low path?

The orderly and dignified exchange of power, the inspiring ceremonial address of the new president, the ex-president's successful negotiations for the release of our people, and his warm acceptance home in Georgia—all these events from yesterday positively affirm the values in a system where people count.

Yesterday, as a Christian and as an American, I felt tall. Great nations behave with greatness. Let's pray that "one nation under God" will have an increased meaning now for everyone, a phrase that will never become empty.

What Role for Government?

June 14, 1981

The budget battle in Washington is more than a financial fight; it involves an ideological question about the role of government. The persistently popular idea that our two political parties are really not very different, and that we should vote for men and not for parties is being shattered in this new political revolution. The Roosevelt years fostered the theory that government is the servant of the people. Simply stated, government is to do things for people. Under this theory, government has grown, agencies have proliferated, many social programs have been established and the taxes have become a heavier and heavier burden.

Now, the opposite theory is on the rise: the best government is the least government. Advocates of this theory say turn the people loose to solve their own problems at personal and local levels. Take the strictures off the business community and it will function efficiently to provide jobs and goods and services in abundance. Dismantle as quickly as possible the social benefit programs; they are not the proper province of government.

These are obviously very simplistic caricatures of the opposing theories of government's role, but they are instructive for my point. And my point is this: Christians do not have a Biblical mandate for either of these views. Such theories about government constitute opinions about a very complex host of problems concerning economics, national defense, responsibility for the poor, legal access to the courts, law enforcement, management of public lands, and on and on. Christians in government do not walk lock-step with their own parties, or with each other, on the way that we should address these problems.

What little information the New Testament gives on the role of government does not help much on these issues. We know from the New Testament that government is essential, that it exercises power to punish law-breakers and can require taxes, and that Christians are to obey the laws of the land. That's about all. We don't find any theory of government, of economics, or of social responsibility on a governmental level.

So before we get at one another's throats on the various ramifications of the changes that are taking place, let's remember that we are citizens of Heaven. Christians are bound together by ties that go beyond any loyalties that we may have to political parties or theories of economics or government.

Only time will tell whether or not the new policies are more successful than the ones they replaced. But it is certainly clear that in this world of rapid change, "business as usual" is impossible.

What Can a Christian Be?

August 16, 1981

Can a Christian be a Republican, a Democrat, a member of the ACLU, the Audubon Society, Sierra Club, Moral Majority, Environmental Action, League of Women Voters, or the Daughters of the American Revolution?

All of these groups have several things in common. They are not the church. They represent certain interest groups in the society. They hold special convictions about America and the world and about where America ought to be headed and how it ought to get there.

Most Christians here in America belong to at least one of these special emphasis groups. We are either Democrats or Republicans, and many of us are members in or supporters of several more of these organizations. It's obvious that, as citizens of this land, we have the privilege and the responsibility to participate in the democratic decision-making process.

The problem is that the range of these decisions and the directions we ought to take are not clearly spelled out in the Bible. Naturally, then, we are not agreed on what the "Christian" decision should be on every policy matter.

Should some of us, then, determine which political party is more Christian, or which special interest group represents the Christian position on the environment, human rights, solar energy, nuclear energy, the voting rights law, and so forth? Well, if we try to do that we will divide the Christian family, because we will be eventually led to withdraw fellowship from those who will not support the "Christian" positions and who are aligned with supporters of "non-Christian" positions.

To be specific on a few issues: some Christians favor ratification of the Equal Rights Amendment, some oppose this; some favor a constitutional prayer amendment, some do not want this; some favor busing for implementing desegregation, others oppose this. The list can easily be lengthened.

Are we to allow differences on these matters to divide brother from brother and sister from sister in the body of Christ? We will allow this to happen if we do not hold fast to the unity that we have in Christ and grant to each other the same right that we want for ourselves to think and decide on such matters.

Troubled, changing times present many problems. Such times test our convictions about the church and about government for, of, and by the people.

Conservative or Liberal?

May 30, 1982

"Can a Christian of conservative Biblical views be a political liberal?" Her question was serious.

My answer: "Of course." Where could anyone get the idea that conservative theology mandated conservative political thinking or vice versa? Where in the Bible are the tenets of conservative or liberal politics discussed as such?

"Well, now, hold on," someone will say, "The principles are there, if you just look for them." Maybe. But I've noticed that we can find "Biblical principles" for almost any idea if we try hard enough. I'm not easily convinced that evidence for party platforms abounds in the Bible.

As a matter of fact, the political conservative-liberal distinctions do not distinguish Christian followers along conservative-liberal theological lines. Geography, family background, economic status, and other forces seem to have more to do with our political slants than do particular ways of looking at the Bible. President Carter, an avowed born-again, Bible-believing, conservative Christian, is a recognized political liberal. President Reagan is also an avowed Christian, but his convictions are a bit less fundamental and his affiliations are a bit more moderate. Yet he is a political conservative. These men read the same Bible.

The terms *conservative* and *liberal* don't stand for the same things politically as they do Biblically. Biblically (and here I am going to oversimplify), we think of conservatives as holding to the Scriptures as God's Word, affirming that Jesus is divine, risen from the dead, and that salvation is totally dependent upon His sacrifice. Liberals tend to be shaky on some or all of these positions. Some liberals completely deny some or all of these conservative convictions. But these are Biblical tenets, not political positions.

Oversimplifying the political definitions as well, may I suggest that conservatives believe that the best government is the least government, that the free market place will stimulate the production of goods and wealth and adequately provide for their distribution, and that taxation is not to be used as an economic equalizer. Liberals believe that government must do things for the people and police the market place and that taxation is a proper method for the equalization of wealth, overcoming some of the disparities between the rich and the poor.

Obviously, Christians can and do hold either of these positions, and some are involved in some mixture of them. We certainly get into the danger of distorting the Bible when we try to maintain that any particular set of political views is a Biblical position.

After all, the way of salvation doesn't include side paths where men may add new requirements after a person has accepted Christ and been baptized. God accepts us as the Bible says; we'd better not reject one another because we differ in matters external to the Bible.

July Fourth and the First Amendment

July 4, 1982

"Congress shall make no law respecting an establishment of religion, or prohibiting the free exercise thereof, or abridging the freedom of speech, or of the press; or the right of the people to assemble, and to petition the government for a redress of grievances."

So goes the First Amendment to the Constitution of the United States. In a lot of places in the world the ideas in that amendment are considered seditionary. Sedition is the incitement of discontent against the government. Obviously, where these First Amendment rights are not enjoyed by the people, those who agitate for them are considered dangerous to the government.

What great power those in authority can wield if they are able to dictate what religion, if any is permissible, who may speak and what they may speak about, what can be published or programmed on radio or TV, and who may or may not assemble. And if the government can remove all access to redress for grievances, then the government has absolute power over the people. That kind of government cannot generally be removed without armed revolution. In a sense, that's what we are remembering on this Fourth of July.

Our founding fathers were well aware of what happens when reasonable petitions on taxation are denied and when protection from unlawful arrest and from unwarranted search and seizure are set aside. They knew the tyranny of unreasonable government, not only in the colonies but in the long, dreary history of monarchies with dictatorial rule.

Attaining those rights is not easy, and keeping them is equally difficult. The fact that we've possessed them here for almost two hundred years is quite remarkable. It is not surprising, understanding the terrific potency of these freedoms, that constant efforts are made to limit, subvert, or modify them.

Inherent in these rights is the power of the people. They protect what Lincoln called government of the people, by the people, and for the people. The emphasis is on *people*. That's the very distinct thing about this grand experiment in democracy that we celebrate today.

What a sad commentary that in the last election about only fifty percent of the people went to the polls. Of course, not all of them voted for Reagan, which means the new administration was chosen by a minority of the citizens of this democracy! Where were the people?

This day must be much more than hot dogs, apple pies, and concerts in the park, and fireworks at the fairgrounds. If we expect to export to others our celebrated brand of democracy, we'd better resolve on this Fourth of July to support this democracy here. And we'd better be alert to the fact that efforts are being put forth all the time to limit the rights for which others have fought and died.

Schools, Religion, and the State

March 27, 1983

I have been reading summations of the important Supreme Court decisions concerning freedom of religion and the separation of church and state. Most of these cases involve public education. Here, more than anywhere else, we seem to be constantly testing the application of the First Amendment. That amendment reads: "Congress shall make no law respecting an establishment of religion or prohibiting the free exercise thereof; or abridging the freedom of speech, or of the press; or the right of the people peaceably to assemble, and to petition the Government for redress of grievances."

In 1952 the Court upheld New York City's public school released-time religious education program. Under this program, students by written permission from their parents could leave the school property to receive religious education during school time.

Earlier, in 1948 the Court ruled that this kind of education could not take place on the school property. The judges claimed that such instruction on the school property would use tax-supported institutions for the promotion of religion in violation of the First Amendment.

In the 1952 decision to allow released-time religious education, the Court held that it was not the intent of the Constitution to establish absolute separation of church and state. Such separation would be impracticable and contrary to the tenets of people whose institutions presuppose a Supreme Being.

Ten years later the Court ruled that school authorities prescribing a prayer violated the First Amendment prohibition.

In 1970 the Court held as constitutional a state law granting tax exemptions on church property. The judges said that this was only a minimal involvement of the state with the church, whereas taxing the property would be a far greater involvement. In effect, the Court recognized that there was no way for absolute non-involvement and opted for the lesser involvement.

While reading through these summaries it seemed to me that the general philosophy of the Court was best illustrated in a decision in 1963. In this decision the Court held it to be unconstitutional to recite the Lord's Prayer and read from the Bible as a part of school opening exercises. But the judges observed that this did not prevent objective study of the Bible or of religions in the schools.

As we engage in a national debate on prayer in the schools, we might find it helpful to sort out (more thoroughly than I have in this article) the actual decisions made by the Supreme Court bearing on this matter.

Although I do not favor an amendment to exclude school prayer cases from the jurisdiction of the Supreme Court, I strongly favor some legislation that would guarantee voluntary religious activities on school property. This would keep the state out of religion without hindering the voluntary exercise of religion.

CHAPTER EIGHT

GOD'S WORLD

In a time when environmentalism has become part of the "politically correct" landscape, it is important to put George Alder's writings on this subject in perspective. He was well ahead of his time in reference to the larger ecological movement. George was known to lament that once again the non-Christian world had trumped the Christian community by co-opting a fundamental Biblical doctrine, namely the stewardship of the earth. George felt that the Christian community was left to catch up by a more perceptive and sensitive world.

The articles that follow do not carry the "catch up" feel but resonate with passion regarding Christian obligations to "dress and keep" the Garden. Never an in your face eco-radical, George nevertheless quietly recycled, produced organically grown food, bicycled when possible, and lived more simply than most. He introduced many of us to Francis Schaeffer's <u>Death and the Pollution of Man</u>, which echoed his own belief that any environmental ethic outside a Biblical frame of reference was merely expedient and would likely result in another round of what is currently called the *culture wars*. For George, sound ecology was sound Biblical thinking. He never would have thought of environmental concerns as reducible to left wing or liberal politics. In George's view, to abuse the natural world was a kind of theft since the world belongs to God and is the product of His handiwork.

George was known to vehemently protest against the presumption that Christians had been the major contributors to the crisis in ecology by applying the Genesis doctrine of "dominion" as a pretext to plunder the earth. He deeply believed that any fair reading of Scripture yielded an ethic of care and stewardship. George believed that God calls human beings to co-operate and participate with Him in the care of the world.

For years he presented sermons, college lectureships and workshops on this topic through the auspices of the Institute for Christian Resources in San Jose, California.

Dominion Over the Earth

February 27, 1972

Not long ago I read that four-tenths of one part of DDT to one billion parts of sea water was sufficient to kill cocktail shrimp. It's hard to imagine how little DDT that is. But if you took one ounce of chocolate syrup (that's one-eighth of a common drinking glass) and put that into milk to make chocolate milk of the same strength as four-tenths of one part DDT to one billion parts of sea water you'd have to mix that syrup into 2,500 railroad tank cars of milk. That would be a trainload of extremely weak chocolate milk about twenty-five miles long.

Today our awakening awareness about ecology is making us more sensitive to the delicate balance of things that God in His providence has created. In the Colossian letter Paul said that all things were created through Jesus and that in Him all things are held together (Colossians 1:17). We know that if He gives such power and personal attention to life, then we cannot be callous toward it. We know that we must become responsible stewards of what He has made and given.

It is true that God gave to man dominion over the earth, but it is not true that such dominion implies the right to plunder and destroy the earth. Realizing that the Creator has organized nature into a delicately balanced system in which man is an integral part leads us to consider seriously our role in His plan. Already we have destroyed many life forms completely and are seriously threatening many others. Great land areas have been laid waste by mining, logging, and unwise farming methods. Waters all over the earth have been polluted, and even the air we breathe is almost intolerable in large industrial centers.

We are living on a great space ship. We must give attention to taking care of this ship, because it is our home. Man's selfish madness is destroying the ship. Christians have theological wisdom to bring to this problem. Political and scientific implementation are essential to change the disastrously destructive course we now follow. This can come about successfully only when men recognize that we are God's servants on earth. This alone can provide the motivation to make the sacrifice necessary to save the ship.

The World Is Ours

May 7, 1972

A Christian ecologist speaking recently at San Jose Bible College reminded us that God told man to "have dominion over the earth." He did not tell man to destroy the earth. We take water and mineral deposits, use them up, and scatter the refuse everywhere. I've seen piles of bottles and cans around mountain lakes and trail junctions in the High Sierras. Every natural sanctuary of wildlife and natural beauty is an object for some speculator who visualizes resorts, vacation homes, ski lifts, hydroelectric plants, or timber and minerals.

In the face of this problem I believe that the key word for Christians is "stewardship." We are stewards of what God has given. Therefore, we share a responsibility for how we use or misuse our environment. Wanton destruction is both stupid and sinful. I suppose most people believe that. What can I do about it? What can you do?

First of all, instead of blaming everyone else (Standard Oil, U.S. Steel, the other campers, etc.), let's recognize that we are personally stewards of what God has given. Second, let's not excuse ourselves by saying, "What little I do can't make any difference anyway." It's the little that many do that will make the difference, and it's the little that we do that teaches our children reverence for the natural world in which God has placed us.

So, the ecologist convinced me that I could save newspapers, cans, and bottles for recycling. I'd already been convinced that biodegradable detergents would help protect the water. And I'm convinced that I can help get rid of air pollution by driving a smaller car, using less fuel, which also protects our fossil fuel deposits. Why burn more than needed and add to the smog?

We Christians, more than anyone else, should be ecology conscious because we know who made the earth good, and we know He expects us to take care of it.

We Are Part of the Environment

November 19, 1972

As early as 1863 George Perkins Marsh of Vermont warned that man is a major biological force threatening his own environment. Few people paid any attention to him or his book, *Man and Nature*. Few people at that time felt any obligation to the environment. Religious thought had been sidetracked four years earlier into a battle with Darwin's theories on the origin of life.

Attention was drawn briefly at least to man's destructiveness during the great dust bowl exodus of the early 1930's. Vast areas of the Great Plains were seriously eroded. But even this was insufficient to awaken our nation or the world to the impending environmental crisis. In 1962 Rachel Carson brilliantly explained what we were doing to our environment in her book, *Silent Spring*. She showed how our massive chemical warfare on insects and microorganisms was upsetting the delicate balance in nature and she also pointed out alternatives to this suicidal attempt to control nature.

Rachel Carson and her book were bombarded by those who were dedicated to the idea that technology would save us. Now we know that she was right and we are beginning to worry about the three hundred to five hundred million pounds of DDT floating around in our atmosphere and being stored up on the fatty tissues of all animal life including man, a time bomb waiting to explode when the body calls on those reserves in an emergency.

In this century more damage has been done to the environment than in all of man's previous history. What should Christians be doing and saying about this? May I suggest that we recognize that we are stewards of the earth; we weren't put here to plunder. We are part of the environment not external to it. Luxury does not provide happiness, but does require exorbitantly high usages of precious materials. And we must be aware that man may solve many problems with science, but science is not God. Our technology is a fragmentary, often dangerous, manipulation of the divine order. Now is the time to study that divine order and cooperate with God. We have fought Him too long.

Balance of Nature?

July 19, 1973

The mental pictures we use for understanding complicated things may at the same time help and hinder our understanding. A case in point is the "balance of nature" picture. Helpfully, this makes us aware that nature has some kind of life equilibrium or "balance" which can get out of whack. It's good that we comprehend that there is danger in deliberately, or accidentally, upsetting this balance.

But this picture can hinder our understanding also. For in things that have balance, a wheel for example, that balance can quite simply be restored if it should be lost. We put the wheel on a machine, determine the amount of weight needed to restore balance, fasten the weights to the wheel and have a wheel running true again. This idea applied to nature may lead us to think that man can rather easily repair damage or imbalance in nature. This just isn't true. Nature is much more complex than this picture of balance suggests.

What if every weight we added to the wheel had the power to deteriorate other portions of the wheel? Then our corrective weights would promote more imbalance and seriously impair and at last destroy our wheel. Once we have overgrazed a steep hillside so that the downward wash of the rains is removing more soil than the decaying rocks can replenish we face an almost irreversible process.

Severe destruction of the deer's predators may provide more game, but also seriously damage plant life. Then we build more roads to bring more hunters to kill the deer and our new predator, man, is far more severe in his onslaught on the tender forest ecology than were the predators he previously destroyed. Other relationships are now disturbed.

Again and again we prove that it is much easier to upset balance than to restore it. Maybe this mental image of balance causes us to think too simplistically about nature. I suggest that we should study "balance" or relationships in nature much more patiently and thoroughly before either altering balance or attempting to restore it. Often our cures prove worse than the disease.

Fire From Heaven

August 17, 1975

Do you remember Prometheus? According to the ancient Greek myth he was of the race of the Titans. He befriended man by bringing fire down from Heaven. With this gift man became more than a match for the animals on earth. He could make weapons and tools to kill or domesticate animals, to cultivate the earth, to warm his house and cook his food, to develop his artistic talents, and, finally, to coin money and establish trade and business.

Zeus was offended by Prometheus' act of kindness, so he chained the Titan to Mount Caucasus and punished him ceaselessly. One of the ironies of this story is that the name Prometheus means "the one who thinks ahead." He was the Titan with foresight; yet even with that gift he was not able to avoid punishment or follow a better course.

Prometheus stands forth as a symbol of the inventive powers of man and also as a symbol of the enslaving results of this inventiveness. The torture of our modern technological age is that we have been able to provide so many creature comforts without getting any closer to peace of mind, love, faith, hope, and other values that we must have to sustain us.

We have learned to control things, but not self. The animals, the earth, the air, the water have all been made subject to man, yet man does not fully control them. We have destroyed many entire species of animals, and presently have many more on the endangered species' list. We have eroded vast amounts of precious soil, polluted most of the rivers, and are even threatening the oceans with our industrial wastes. The air has become a great conveyer belt carrying noxious gases and chemical dust particles from our factories to even the most remote places on the earth.

Like Prometheus we land on Mount Caucasus. Only as we accept the sacrifice of Him who hung on Mount Calvary can we learn to turn from our courtship with death to a genuine love of life. The Greeks had only Prometheus, and they sounded the warning. We have Jesus; we have the answer!

We Have Met the Enemy

March 28, 1976

I've spotted his tracks in many places. I've walked along a beautiful mountain trail and found a heap of trash at a junction. I've seen beer cans in trout streams, avoided broken glass on a bicycle path, choked on fumes in a traffic jam, stopped to get a drink along a lakeshore and found decomposing food in the water.

Along the roads and highways, I've seen paper, boxes, old discarded cans, and dead animals. As Pogo put it, "We have met the enemy and he is us!" The massive amount of stuff that we produce and discard would leave fewer marks if we were more careful in disposal.

Why did those kids drop the soft drink cans on my yard, and when asked to pick them up act surly, take the cans and drop them in the street a hundred feet away? Why did the young trees put in the parking strip in front of the telephone building and along a vacant frontage get broken off time after time? Why did a nice looking man in a fine car open the door and dump the cigarette butts from his ashtray in the restaurant parking lot?

Do we scatter junk around in our living room? Do we have rotting food in the sink, and broken glass on bedroom floors? Do we want every trail, every stream and lake, every road and every field to be a junk yard and a place for filth?

But we are the enemy. We meet ourselves all the time. Men must come to know that the earth is the Lord's, and that we must honor His property and respect the home He gave us. Cleanliness and beauty are everybody's job.

Economics and Ecology

July 11, 1976

Economics and ecology have one common linguistic root, so the words are cousins. That common root "Eco" comes from the Greek word meaning "house." So economics and ecology both relate to our house or home here on earth. But the words are sharply divergent in their final roots and so become sharply different in usage. "Economics" is completed with a Greek root "nom," which means "law." "Ecology" is completed with the root "log," which means "word." As often used it means "the science of, or study of" something.

Economics (the laws of the house) has to do with the ways we handle income, gain it, use it, distribute it. It deals largely with our financial concerns. Ecology is the science of all relationships between life and environment.

Now we have great stresses between economic interests and ecological interests. Obviously a national forest has a lot of valuable timber when thought of in economic terms. But in ecological terms the timber may also be very valuable as a part of the life-support system for many plants and animals, as a protection to a watershed upon which lower valleys depend for running streams in summer, and for enjoyment of people who find wilderness an important personal value.

Gold in the side of a mountain may be mined by washing the mountainside off with high pressure water jets. Gold is an economically sound value. But the destroyed mountainside and the stream that is filled with gravel, sand, and boulders may be important ecological values.

Until we learn to find our guiding value system in the relation of life with environment, we shall continue to allow economics to dominate. Instead of caring for the earth as stewards, we have become self-seeking masters seeking short-term gains regardless of the future. A day of accounting will come.

Where Did the Buffalo Go?

September 19, 1976

I was amazed to read in James L. Haley's book, *The Buffalo War*, about the destruction of the buffalo in the last quarter of the nineteenth century. Haley documents from the records of the military commander at Dodge City that 750,000 hides were shipped out in 1873. The figure for three years, 1872-74 is 4,373,730 buffalo killed. This carnage destroyed the buffalo herds in a few years.

One motivation was quick profit from the hides. The other was that the Plains Indians would be forced to go on reservations if their food supply was destroyed. Only in recent years have any sizeable herds of buffalo been developed from the remnant of the species.

Probably this destruction, linked as it was to human destruction, stands out as an example of man's ruthlessness with nature. The great buffalo herds were an abundant source of food from the prairies. When they were replaced by domestic animals and much of the land was tilled to raise grain, a more complex economic chain was developed and the ecological balance was broken. Now, though human demand for protein is growing, it becomes more and more unsound to feed grain products to domestic animals to produce meat protein. This process is very wasteful. Now a new breed of meat animals, the beefalo, utilizes the capacity of the buffalo to produce protein from grass. There are some who predict that this will lead to cheaper and more abundant meat as well as more grain products for human consumption.

It has taken us about a hundred years to leave the buffalo and then turn back to him again. This should remind us that the destruction of any species for immediate profit may be a most costly mistake, whether man ever recognizes this or not.

WATER!

January 30, 1977

If the world were the size of an egg (can you imagine this?), then all the water on the world would amount to just one drop! Can you imagine *that*? At first one is inclined to say, "No, that can't be right." A little careful thinking will make us realize that the earth is eight thousand miles in diameter and the water on it is a very, very thin layer. If the earth were the size of an egg, the mass of all the water would be just one drop.

And this is why devastating oil spills, factory pollution in rivers, sewage disposal in streams and lakes and in the ocean, and other wasteful usage of water is dangerous. Life on the earth depends upon water; it is the solvent that makes living things live. Remove it and death comes soon.

But we have looked at the supply of water as so great that nothing we could do could harm it. We have seen the ocean as endless, but it is just a big lake; the biggest one we have, that's true, but it is not endless.

Now we are becoming more conscious of the role of water in our lives. This means that we are becoming more aware of our relation to the earth. The earth is our home. From the beginning of man's existence, God assigned him the role of steward. He was never made to be an exploiter. Would God assign man the role of destroyer of his own home?

That image of the earth as an egg and water as a drop suggests the delicate relationship of living things to the natural environment. We had better put a high priority on preserving this relationship. Sooner or later we must give an account of our stewardship.

What Is Conservation All About?

July 8, 1979

I'm sure that the word *conservation* stirs up a whole host of ideas in our minds. We think of environmental groups trying to protect endangered species or farmers trying to save soil on eroding farmlands or ourselves driving slower to save fuel or our children collecting cans and bottles to recycle. We conserve because of some feeling of need. And we are more aware now than ever of our power to use up, discard, and destroy.

The environment we share with animals and plants makes life possible for all living things. We human beings, a minority species until recently in history, are now the most threatening, destructive, and demanding portion of the life that shares our earth.

Life around us generally does not have the capacity to adapt to us; we are too intelligent, inventive, and powerful. Our heavy equipment, guns, nets, poisons, and generic know-how may place intolerable burdens on life around us.

But we also depend upon this life. We must have plants; otherwise we would not have oxygen to breathe or food to eat. Even if nature held no aesthetic fascination for us, we would still be dependent upon the life system it provides.

This raises the question of conservation. Must we save anything? Can we simply destroy all life on earth? Possibly. But then we are dead, too. Can we save absolutely everything? Probably not. We take up room and are competitors—with other life forms—for land, water, air, and food.

We can act responsibly, however, to share, protect, and even enhance the life-giving properties of our garden, the earth. So we are the ones assigned by God as His gardeners, His conservators. We must use our wisdom to fit in with and adapt ourselves to the garden. That's what conservation is all about.

Longages Not Shortages

July 29, 1979

Dr. Garett Hardin of the University of California argues that we do not have shortages on earth, only a "longage" of people. This is perfectly obvious. If the world population were say a ridiculously small 500,000 people, the abundance of food and space would not even be dented by such a few. But if we continue to multiply the number of people, there must come a time when the resources become insufficient. The system will then balance by starvation, disease, and warfare.

When God made the earth He made a closed system. Everything is here that He intended to be here. We have water, iron, air, soil, gold, and all the rest. Many resources that we have are used over and over again. Water, for example, is recycled constantly. We can also recycle metals again and again. However, some resources are not renewable for us. Once we've used up a tank of gasoline we have no way to reclaim it again.

On our farm when I was a boy we could sustain only so many cattle on our pastureland. If we tried to keep too many there, they ruined the pasture. There is always a balance between resources and demands placed upon them.

Our first task as a human family was to tend the garden, to keep it, to care for it. That is still our task. It is a spiritual responsibility, a stewardship before the Lord. Our ruthless exploitation of the earth will pay us back with what appear to be shortages. The real problem is that we are asking too much; we have created many "longages."

God has given us all that we need here. But we have the capacity for misuse as well as for temperance, stewardship, and good management. Let's not criticize the Creator by shouting "shortage" when the real problem is with us.

"The Gas Glut Worsens!"

May 3, 1981

The gas glut worsens! Can you imagine that? That was the evaluation given on the news tonight over a local TV station. After explaining that the car dealers had sold more than 2,800 cars in the first half of February, a very great increase over previous months, the newsman discussed the national gasoline situation. He told us that the refineries had their storage tanks full, that the delivery lines were full and that "the gas glut worsens," I was startled. I immediately wrote down his words.

Shouldn't we be saying "the gas glut betters," or maybe something more grammatical such as, "Since we are using less gasoline, the supply is abundant"? Four years ago President Carter warned that the energy battle was the moral equivalent of war. Why should we think that the situation worsens when we use less and the tanks get full? Are we so caught up in consumerism that we can see nothing optimistic in the success of conservation?

The less gasoline we use, the less we must depend upon foreign supplies and long shipping distances across the oceans. The less we use now, the more we will have left for the future. The less we use here, the more likely it is that the price may drop enough so that poor countries—deficient in energy and fertilizer—may be able to supply their need.

It should encourage us whenever we learn to use the products of the earth with efficiency, temperance, and wisdom.

Several years ago in California there was a severe water shortage; the rains did not come for two years. Appeals were made to the public to conserve. The conservation effort was so successful that in some areas consumption dropped almost 50 percent. At least one water company wanted to raise the price of water delivered to compensate for the loss of revenue!

In this situation in California, the supply depended entirely on when the rains would come again. There was no way to develop a glut of water.

We are still having a hard time realizing that many things that we use are non-renewable. We have no way, for example, of putting oil back into the earth again. When the oil is gone, it's gone, that's all. So when we learn to be careful, we ought to be encouraged. The gas glut may be getting better. Unfortunately, short term oversupplies do not prophesy a future of plenty.

CHAPTER NINE

THE SEASONS

In one of his reflections from this section, George presents a striking challenge. He calls for a moratorium on Christmas. There is more seriousness than irony in George's message. To no one's surprise George challenges us to bring a halt to Christmas, as we currently know it. What is surprising is that little heed is given to his timeless admonitions.

George was genuinely concerned by the way the Christian message had been muted in the secular celebration of Christmas. He laments the fact that just when Christ is emphasized the most, he may be recognized the least.

What worried George about the secular appropriation of Christmas paralleled his concerns for other distinctly Christian seasons. He was concerned that believers and unbelievers alike had learned to settle for poor copies of the distinctly religious nature of most of our holidays. George believed that losing sight of the first purpose of the seasons impoverishes our lives.

For example, we can fall short of the real purpose of Thanksgiving by being thankful for good health, good fortune, or true friends—while forgetting to whom we should be thankful. Or perhaps Easter is reduced to the celebration of eggs and bunnies rather than the new life found in the resurrection of Jesus. For George, the seasons find their best and most robust expression in the life of faith. While non-believers certainly have a hint of the magic and power of our traditional holidays, they must settle for weak substitutes compared to the fullest sense of their primary meaning. In this section, George's basic concern is to elevate the seasons to their appropriate loftiness so believers might more fully experience the presence of God and unbelievers might find it for the first time.

The Sound of Christmas

December 3, 1972

Already we are hearing the sounds of Christmas. Children are asking for things. Parents are struggling with finances and social pressures. Industry has massed a gigantic advertising campaign to link a bewildering array of products with happiness on Christmas Day. We can hear "Silent Night" blaring out over loudspeakers above the noise of the pressing crowds in supermarkets and department stores. Soon we'll hear the "clop-clop-clop-clop" of helicopters bring scores of Santa Clauses to scores of store parking lots with advice to be "good children" and "print your names clearly on your letters for Santa's mailbox."

With this kind of encouragement anyone can become a cynic quickly. We may want to stop sending cards, give up on gifts, refuse to play the community game of "My house has more lights than your house," and maybe just declare an indefinite moratorium on Christmas.

Can Christmas be better than this? Of course it can. Of course it is for Christians who know what it is all about and who prepare to celebrate His birth with genuine joy. Through all the racket of this busy season His voice can be heard by those who listen. Even in this rush, He will find a place in many hearts, some for the first time. Deeds of love and mercy, even sacrifice, will come from lives that have often been pinched and self-seeking.

Christmas will be what we make it. Either we play the world's games, trade gifts, outdo others, have the biggest tree, or we will hear His voice in this time like a benediction in a world that almost completely ignores God. There were no lights or gifts or trees when He was born. The world was so busy that there was no place for Him in any hotel in Bethlehem.

Some shepherds heard the angelic choir. That choir still sings for those who will listen. Anyone who pauses in the rush can hear that true sound of Christmas. Jesus is born.

Reflections on Thanksgiving Day

November 18, 1973

The nostalgia that moves upon me at Thanksgiving time reminds me that being reared on a farm in the twenties and thirties was a privilege and a blessing in my life. I can identify somewhat with those Pilgrims who on a December day in 1621 gathered to give thanks to God for their harvest. In those little country schools where I got my grade school education we always decorated for Thanksgiving. We made Pilgrims and turkeys out of black paper and put them in the windows. And we read the story about the hard winter and the bountiful harvest.

In those days most of our food came from our farm. Our smokehouse was full of meat. Mother had shelves laden with canned fruits, jams and jellies, and marvelous apple butter. The cellar was filled with apples, pears, pumpkins, squash, carrots, and potatoes. And we even had flour made from our own wheat. Our eggs, butter, and milk had never seen a store. Our Thanksgiving turkey was a native of our farm.

All of this helped me to understand the Pilgrims and added to our festive Thanksgiving Day. The tempting aroma of fresh bread, pumpkin pies, and sage dressing brought our family around the table in a joyous mood. Those were pre-television, pre-football mania Thanksgiving Days.

But one important ingredient was missing. We weren't Christians in those days. We didn't pray. We didn't thank God. Our thankfulness was only a general feeling of appreciation for what we had—a respect for what the earth produced. So just being close to the soil, as wonderfully satisfying as that can be, doesn't guarantee that we'll have God in our lives.

A depression, financial destruction, a move to town, and finding the Lord added that missing ingredient in our home and in our Thanksgiving Day. Knowing God through Jesus Christ led us beyond that vague feeling of appreciation to personal heartfelt gratitude to God for all His blessings.

So the turkey, pies, and all that graces our table now continue to awaken an old nostalgia for days that will never be again. That old nostalgia refreshes us with a sense of wonder and praise that increases from year to year.

Sleep in Heavenly Peace

December 9, 1973

In a delightful little book, *Semantics and Communication*, John C. Condon, Jr., tells a story about his little niece and nephew and their favorite Christmas song, "Silent Night." One day they were singing their carol, and the little boy finished the song "Sleep in heavenly beans." Immediately his little sister corrected him, "not beans, peas!"

From a semantic point of view this illustrates the fact that we hear things and experience things pretty much on the basis of what we have already experienced. It's amusing to think of a field of heavenly peas. In fact, that's a kind of lovely picture for those who have seen a field of peas in full bloom.

It's very easy to feel indulgently superior to children who have such limited experiences that they sing "heavenly beans" or "heavenly peas." But, really now, how complete or satisfactory is our understanding of "heavenly peace"? How many of us know what that is? Can we describe it or demonstrate it or feel it? How much experience do we have to support a clear appreciate of "heavenly peace"? After all, one can see beans and peas, smell them, touch them, and eat them.

Well, if anyone should know what heavenly peace is, we Christians should. Jesus came to give us that peace. He came to relate us to Heaven. He came to relieve us of the burden of sin. He came to renew in us the image of God in which we were made. He came to restore our broken relationship with our heavenly Father.

At Christmas time we all feel the tension between a troubled, sinful, struggling world and His peace. Christians can sing realistically about that peace because in Jesus we have experienced it. Without Him it's a bean field of some sort.

What Kind of New Year?

December 30, 1973

Two words in the Greek New Testament are translated "new." One of these words means new in point of time. For example, any article of clothing, a coat or suit or sweater, is new when we first buy it. Not long after that it's becoming old. A house is new only for a short while, and a car is getting old as soon as you drive it off the lot. It's a "used car" right away.

The other word translated "new" means new in quality. Se we are told in the New Testament about the "new name" (Revelation 2:17), the "new Jerusalem" (Revelation 3:12), the "new heaven and new earth" (Revelation 21:1) and the "new man" (Ephesians 4:24). Perhaps the most impressive example of the use of this word is in "New Testament" or "new covenant" as contrasted with the nature of the old covenant of laws, rituals, ordinances and a sanctuary of this world.

Which of these words will we apply to 1974? Of course, every new year is new in point of time as is every day of one's life. The real question about life is whether we can find a quality of newness in the hours and days and the years or will we settle down into boring monotony? Paul says that "but though our outward man perish, yet the inward man is renewed day by day" (2 Corinthians 4:16). That means that the Christian life can be vitally new all the time! Paul goes on to say that "if any man is in Christ he is a new creature" (2 Corinthians 5:17).

This new life in Jesus can make a new year really new. But 1974 can be old right away unless there is something in us that is new. For many, January 1 will be an old day ushering in an already worn out, monotonous year because the party wasn't new at all, just the same old crowd doing the same old things.

Give Thanks

November 24, 1974

So what are we thankful for this Thanksgiving? What if we had to make lists before we carved the turkey? What would you write down?

It wouldn't be so hard to start out on negative ground: "Lord, I'm thankful that we're not starving like people are in Africa, and thankful, too, Lord, that I've got my health (someone keeps saying that that's just about everything), and I'm thankful that I live in a democracy—most of the people in the world don't have this privilege," etc.

The Pharisees were good at this kind of thanksgiving. They criticized Gentiles, women, and slaves in their litany of praise to God. Their standard prayer was, "Blessed be you, O God, our King, that you did not create me a Gentile, a slave, or a woman." Jesus told a story about one of them who prayed, "I thank you, Lord that I am not greedy, dishonest, or immoral, like everybody else; I thank you that I am not like that tax collector. I fast two days every week, and give you one tenth of my income" (Luke 18:11, 12, *Today's English Version*).

That's more bragging than it is praying. What kind of thanks is it when we are motivated only by the misfortunes of others? As a boy how many times I was told, "There are millions of little Chinese boys..." and this was supposed to make me eat spinach or something.

Real thanksgiving is positive. We ought to see what God has done for us, not just by comparison, but just because He's done it. Otherwise we get caught in religious jargon that's not much more than self-praise or put-down-the-unfortunate.

So gather around the table. Bring on the bird, the potatoes, salad, corn, and everything. See all these as symbolic of His divine protection, and rejoice and give thanks, for the Lord is good!

When I Was a Child

December 19, 1976

From somewhere I recall these poetic lines: "Backward, turn backward, O Time in thy flight; Make me a child again, just for tonight." Many of us adults will engage that nostalgia on Christmas Eve as we dream back across the Christmases that will never be again.

I suspect that for most of us that longing is directed to the wonder and excitement that we knew as children, to those times when we spoke, thought, and reasoned as children. But though we have put off much of our childish traits we cannot easily trade our adult views of Christmas for the childish ones we once had.

Could it be that children are inherently more adaptable to the true meaning of Christmas than adults are? I recall dark times in the great depression of the early thirties. My sister and I had two nickels with which to buy a Christmas present for our little brother. I rode my horse on a snow-covered road from our farm two miles to a little country store to buy a bag of marbles for our brother. His delight with that small gift on Christmas morning confirmed in us the importance of the love which bound our poor family together and which sustained us in traumatic times.

When I was a child I did not know the cynicism of an adult world. I did not know its selfishness, its crass materialism, nor its downright perversion of the beautiful event that made Christmas. When I was a child I felt fully the glow of the love that sent Jesus, but did not know the threat that this infant held for worldly kings and worldly ways.

Because when I was a child I could not know the deep significance of His birth. Sadder and wiser with age I know now that He's the Savior, sent to rescue adults from their childish and foolish ways.

"I'm Just Thankful"

November 20, 1977

Can it be that a person is just thankful? Nothing more than that, just thankful? Imagine this scene: a daughter comes into the house beaming, happy, downright joyful, and her parents ask, "What's going on, what's so great?" Her reply, "I'm in love." Their next question is "With whom?" And she answers, "With no one; I'm just in love."

You could duplicate that little imaginary scene with a person being "just angry," "just afraid," "just ashamed" or just a lot of things. But in all of these situations we know that these terms need some object. We love someone; we're afraid of something; we're angry at someone or something and so forth.

Nevertheless, at this season of the year we'll hear a lot of people say "I'm just so thankful." Then maybe they'll say "I'm thankful for my health," or "I'm thankful for my family" or maybe "I'm thankful that I'm an American." The real question to raise is "To whom are you thankful?" We aren't just thankful; we have to be thankful to someone.

Thanks implies appreciation and an offering of words, things, or actions that show this to be true. If a person has ruled God out of his thinking and his life then he has no one to be thankful to in any ultimate religious way. He may be thankful to himself, his government, his race or whatever, but that isn't the Thanksgiving that was offered by the pilgrims, nor the Thanksgiving that is traditional in our national holiday.

So Thursday let's be more than "Just thankful." Let's praise God the maker of Heaven and earth and all that in them is. Let everything that has a voice praise the Lord!

I Shouldn't Have Eaten So Much!

November 19, 1978

As we draw near to the time when American affluence is nationally celebrated in an official Thanksgiving Day, we might well reflect on the cost of our affluence to others in the world. Food production in the world is directly geared to fertilizer usage. Average world fertilizer usage in 1972 was forty-four pounds per person. In desperately hungry India, though, only ten pounds of fertilizer per person was available and used. By contrast, we used 120 pounds per person that year!

Now, as you may know, most of that fertilizer is a by-product of petroleum products, so food production is linked directly to how much oil a nation can afford. In the simplest terms, the reason poor people do not eat in fancy restaurants is that they don't have the money to do so. People in deprived nations don't eat well because they can't buy food.

The United States in the eyes of these starving people is an economically off limits fancy restaurant. Food abounds here. We can afford to import great quantities of oil to make fertilizer to offset the soil depletion of our huge harvests. We sell surpluses to nations wealthy enough to buy them.

Our well spread Thanksgiving tables do not come about just because of the productivity of the United States, but depend also on energy we purchase from others. And though all things come from God, He has not evenly distributed His bounties everywhere.

So eating well and giving thanks might be tempered with a sense of the awesome responsibility that affluence and productivity bring. Jesus made it plain that in the judgment we would be known by how we treated the naked, the ill, the imprisoned, and the hungry.

If we stop our feasting with "I shouldn't have eaten so much," that's probably more true than we think.

December Again!!

December 3, 1978

It is that time again. The constant barrage of "O Come All Ye Faithful," "O Little Town of Bethlehem" and "Silent Night" will not let us forget for a moment that this is December. It's hard to understand why a society so dedicated to leaving Jesus out of almost everything (His church included) should maintain such a love affair with Christmas. But why not? We have a love affair with football, prize fights, soap operas, game shows, off-color comedy, and a lot of other time-consuming pastimes promoted by the hucksters of our culture.

We are reminded in this month more than in any other that there is a sharp contrast between who Jesus is and what our world advertises Him to be. Stores filled with things, advertising that makes you feel it is impossible to be happy without that stuff, and a merry mixture of the baby, Santa, Wise-men and alcoholic concoctions paint a picture of sentimentality, materialism, religion, and personal indulgence. And so, just when Jesus is emphasized the most, He may be recognized the least.

Now I know that the acceptable way to finish such a criticism of our national sacred day would be with some positive affirmation of all the good that is done at this time. But I have a deeper concern. Can we who know Him untangle ourselves from the pagan, non-Christian values that a mercantile world presents under the guise of His birthday celebration, and actually find Him in Bethlehem's manger? Will we so demonstrate His love and sacrifice at this season that others may see Him and come to love Him even at Christmas time?

Making the New Year New

December 28, 1980

Each year is a new year. But whether or not it is new for us in anything but time depends upon what we do with it. Years in human life always mark off for us a sequence of time elements (days and weeks and months) but not necessarily a sequence of growth or progress elements in our own experience.

The celebration of a year gone and a new year arriving reveals that deep concern we all share to be going somewhere, to be making progress. In some sense for all of us it is also a point marking the putting aside of failures, disappointments, heartaches, broken promises, unkept resolutions, and the weaknesses in character that fill us with guilt.

Actually, we know that there is not one whit of power available to us at 12:01 A.M. January 1 that was not available to us before that moment. We know that there is no magic in that moment to erase our sins or renovate our lives. But this chronological changing point for planet earth has traditionally offered to us a personal changing point as well.

How can the year be new for you and me? I happen to believe in making resolutions. I like the beginning of the new year as a time to reorder my life, to set priorities, and to measure where I've been weak and where I've been strong.

As Christians we know that repentance means a change of mind and action. Certainly, we don't wait for January 1 to make amends for wrongs, to seek forgiveness, or to determine on a more Christ-centered way of life. But at this season, like a sailor at sea, we can use our spiritual sextant to take our position from the Son of God and then plot out a course for the year ahead.

Unless we do this periodically, even more often than once a year, we may wander off course, even drift away from the salvation and safety He alone affords.

What a blessing 1981 can be if it becomes for us a time that is really new, not just a new time period but a new life period. I feel like celebrating that hope for the future.

Proverbs Personally Distilled for 1984

January 1, 1984

There is nothing very much new or original under the sun. What follows is my rewriting of some ideas from Proverbs to set my feet on the right path for the new year. I hope this may be of some guidance for you as well.

There are many voices calling out, "This is the way." Therefore, I must be careful to listen for His voice and trust His guidance.

My mind is His gift. Its complexities are beyond my imagination. What I do with my mind is my stewardship. Bad thinking makes for bad living.

I am not even close to being infinitely wise. I need all the good advice I can get. I must have the humility to listen to those who are wiser than myself.

This year will have only a regularly allotted number of days. I will be a stupid person if I waste my days on useless projects. Lord, I need to know how to set priorities.

I've never been rich nor have I been driven to the depths of poverty. I must remember that God expects me to use my energies responsibly. If I become lazy, I deserve to be impoverished.

All of us contrive to manipulate our environment for our advantage. These are our plans. I must not forget that these are human efforts. Events are directed by the Lord, not by me.

The temptation to know the answer, to be the teacher of others, the wise one, is a powerful temptation. It is wiser to listen carefully and do some thinking before speaking up. Stupidity and pride are revealed by talking.

If I am to be victimized by wanting, then all I must do is to want for more and more. My desires, unchecked, will make me a slave to a world of things. Covetousness is idolatry.

There are foolish people who talk on TV, write books, make films, and send out cassettes. Foolish people cannot teach me anything worthwhile. 1984 will be too short to waste my time on foolishness.

It's easy to act big and cling to pride. I'll be much wiser to trust in God's strength and walk in humility.

Best wishes for 1984!

A Letter to Mom

May 13, 1984

Dear Mom,

I've put off writing this letter almost forever. I wonder what my life would have been if you had put off doing for me all the things you did while I was growing up. Surely I would have starved or died of illness before I got through school, if it hadn't been for you.

Mom, it doesn't take long for me to come to the edge of my emotions when I begin remembering the things that I took for granted years ago. So many times I timed my entrance into the house just at the moment that you took the freshly baked bread from the oven along with that extra pan of cinnamon rolls (the gooey ones) that I always found so yummy. I was encouraged when you would take my report card and say, "Oh, this is wonderful, better than last time. I'm proud of you." And you kept my clothes clean and mended and you scrubbed me, too, even when I had that too-close encounter with the pretty black-and-white striped kitty down by the barn. I think you buried my clothes that time!

Remember the Christmas when all we kids had chicken pox, and I got the new sled? You took the sled and tried it out by the window so I could see that it would really slide in the snow.

Those tough years with so little money and hardly any conveniences at all had to be very hard for you. I didn't know it then. I didn't realize how many things I take for granted now that you just did without: indoor plumbing, washing machine, electricity, and the freedom to get into the car and drive away somewhere. I suppose these were just dreams of luxuries that you never expected to have.

I understand now that you were a young woman when I was growing up, giving your youthful years to me and the rest of the kids and to Dad as well.

Mother's Days of years ago were made special for you by such little things. Remember how I spilled your coffee, bringing it up the stairs to show you how I loved you when I was only five? And then there was the time when we kids pooled all our savings to get you a corsage. How proud we were to see our mom in church on Mother's Day wearing flowers.

We always seemed to fumble a bit in trying to say what our hearts really felt. We still fumble a bit when we try to tell you how much we love you.

So, Mom, when I see you again, I want to hold you close and tell you with all my heart, "I love you."

CHAPTER TEN

MORTALITY AND HOPE

It couldn't be true! Not George Alder!! The man who sometimes grew food organically, composted, recycled, rode a bicycle when possible, backpacked into his late fifties, and kept himself so fit. We raged at the idea someone so valuable, so loved, so needed, with so much yet to give, could be taken so early. It wasn't fair! We were angry with God—for the moment. Then it began to dawn: The mentor, teacher, father, friend had one last lesson for us—pointing us in rudimentary and calm simplicity back to our faith, God and hope. George was dying of prostate cancer and he knew it. We cried, we prayed, and we hoped it would not come true—but it did! We found it necessary to return to what we had learned most clearly from our mentor-teacher—that this is truly God's world, that we are privileged to live in it and enjoy it for a while—a testimony to the delicate ecology of life and death, hope and despair, joy and pain—which is life itself. The three articles which follow display grace and courage by which George could write about his own mortality. His "Ten Principles to Live By in 1985" constitute a wonderful summative testimony of his faith in the Gospel of Christ which so defined his life.

The Sweetest Balm

April 22, 1984

Nothing can excite enthusiasm for the resurrection more than the announcement many receive (I, too, have received it), "Your disease is incurable." If one had doubted the reality of personal, physical mortality, or its nearness, or its power before hearing these words, all that is blasted away in just one breath in that single sentence from the oncologist, "Your disease is incurable."

Today will be for me one of the most spiritually exhilarating days of my whole life. Of course, I know and have taught for years that Christians need no special, annual day for remembering Christ's resurrection; every Lord's Day is resurrection day for us. But having said that, I know and you know that He was raised on one special Sunday morning in one special year and that Easter is a way for us to celebrate that great, triumphal event.

If we could momentarily imagine with great clarity the phenomenal organization of matter and energy that constitute each human being, at that moment we would want to celebrate forever the miracle of creation that makes each of us unique and alive. To know in faith that no disintegration of this structure can destroy the personality that dwells in our earthly tabernacle makes any human celebration, exalted as it may be, but a paltry praise to Him who was dead and is alive forever.

Dressed today in our best earthly garments, worshipping in meetinghouses garlanded with spring's fairest blossoms, hearing and singing together the great songs of victory, and thrilling with the pulpit proclamation, "He is risen!" we taste gently of that blessed hope.

For Christians, His victory and the promise of our participation with Him in that victory serve as the sweetest balm we can feel upon our wounds when we are told, "Your disease is incurable."

Not the Why but the What

September 15, 1985

Twenty years ago when one of our daughters was terribly, almost mortally ill, Eileen and I received all kinds of information and evaluations about her illness. Some people were sure we ought to know why a twelve-year-old girl was so sick. Now that I'm mortally ill (according to my doctors), I struggle again with this problem of disease, debilitation, and death. Why am I ill? And is that really the important question?

If that *is* the important question, then in this life we must despair of ever finding the answer. Oh, I know, people give answers, but these are only human answers, human judgments, not divine revelation. And the human answers are inconsistent; there is no agreement about the why. I'll never really know why children are born deformed, nor why I see toddlers with cancer at the oncology department where I go for treatment.

Job's friends had their cruel, simplistic answers. Mainly Job heard, "You've done wrong; now you must suffer." Even Job's wife urged him to "curse God and die." Jesus commented on a disaster in His time where eighteen people had been killed when a tower fell. "Do you suppose," He said, "that those eighteen ... were worse culprits than all the men who live in Jerusalem? I tell you, no, but unless you repent, you will all likewise perish" (Luke 13:4,5, *New American Standard Bible*).

Jesus didn't explain why what had happened had happened, but His concern seemed to be in the human reaction to the event. Would the living consider the issues of life, death, righteousness, and evil?

We perish not because of events or diseases that kill us but because of failed relationships with God. It's not so important then, what happens to us. What is important is what we do about it, think about it, and feel about it.

The big question is not, for example, why many of us perish with cancer, but what quality of life such a test produces in us. Do we curse God? Do we hate His world? Do we bemoan our fate? Or can we learn in such situations that God is love, that His world is good but cursed by sin, and that we are not fated to something but rather fulfilling something in an ultimate pattern?

I must consider cancer as an incident in life that has nothing to do with His goodness at all. My faith and relationship to God can be destroyed by the experience if I dwell on the *why*. Once I concentrate on *what* I must do to endure and to grow, then my relationship to God through Christ can become stronger in every trial.

Ten Principles for 1985

December 30, 1984

Now is the time for finalizing our resolutions or thoughts for the new year. Like you, I've been sorting things out a bit and trying to distill my Christian experience and judgment into priorities or principles for 1985. Let me share with you what I feel must guide my life in this next year—my ten principles to live by.

1. Try to incorporate some silence, reflection, and prayer into each day. Walk quietly in the midst of noise, haste, and confusion, allowing God to heal and soothe life with His peace.

2. Put people above things always. Sacrifices and efforts made to develop and keep friendships preserve for us one of life's most precious treasures.

3. Become a complete steward and be faithful in caring for all that God puts within one's trust. Honor God in everything and in every task, regardless of how humble these may seem to be.

4. Recognize that each life is precious in His sight, is in our keeping only for a little while, and counts for something in the changing fortunes of time.

5. Access to the Father in Jesus' name is more valuable than any key to any house, safe deposit box, automobile, summer home, or yacht. We come into His presence in our human poverty and receive from Him blessings manifold.

6. Caring is more important than having or talking. When we love as He has loved us, we become His conduits for blessings to others.

7. Even when our bodies are wearing out and are beset by pain, and life itself is tortured by diminished abilities, we are still His children, still precious in His sight and the subjects of His grace.

8. Where we go, whom we talk with, what we hear and see, and what we eat and drink can either strengthen the human spirit or weaken it. Personal discipline is a part of our stewardship.

9. Cynicism, negativism, and fear are the enemies of happiness, faith, joy, and godliness. It is the mission of every Christian to share the gospel, the great good news, out of an abundant life.

10. No one can make anyone else different than he is. Only by accepting God's power for change can we be transformed day by day into wholeness in the likeness of Jesus our Lord.

www.ingramcontent.com/pod-product-compliance
Lightning Source LLC
Chambersburg PA
CBHW051932160426
43198CB00012B/2127